Woo-Woo

Woo-Woo

Becoming a psychic at fifty

Janet E. Alm, Ph.D.

Janet E. Alm

Mattawan, MI

133.8
alm

Alm, Janet E. (Janet Elaine), 1952-
    Woo-woo : becoming a psychic at fifty / Janet E. Alm.
        p. cm.
    ISBN 978-0-557-29173-1
    1. Alm, Janet E. (Janet Elaine), 1952- 2. Psychics – United States – Biography. 3. Mediums –
United States – Biography. 4. Animal communicators – United States – Biography. 5. Healers –
United States – Biography. 6. Channeling (Spiritualism)

BF1031.A46 2010

Cataloging by the author.

Cover photo by Greg Zimmerman: *Jan Alm feeding redpolls, Fairbanks 2005.*

Janet Alm's website: www.janetalm.com

INTRODUCTION

I used to have a personal policy never to tell a new acquaintance I was a librarian until I'd had the chance to establish myself as a rational human being. Imagine my dismay when, thanks to my dearly departed mother getting in touch from the Other Side, I became a medium. It's pretty much a toss-up which kills the conversation faster, telling someone you're a librarian or a psychic medium.

I never wanted to be a librarian. I blame my old puppeteering partner, Susie, who broke up our act to become a waitress. She left, and I ended up with a career in librarianship. I never wanted to be a medium, either, but I blame Mom for that one. I was fifty, and Mom was dead and gone four years when she suddenly started sending me messages from the Other Side. Now I'm a librarian *and* a medium, and I confess I find both slightly embarrassing.

A friend once described finding books about the famous medium Edgar Cayce in a family attic when she was young. Then she added, "And I've been into woo-woo stuff ever since." What a perfect, tongue-in-cheek description for something at once so mysterious, so wonderful, and ever-so-slightly embarrassing.

1

A re you happy?" the voice asked, and my mind shot back, *Absolutely not*. I looked around to be sure the older man with the New York accent wasn't actually talking to me. A young couple several rows back were sound asleep. Two women at the front of the bus were deep in conversation, and across from them a young mother nodded over an infant in her arms. I checked behind me again and saw only the sleeping couple. That was it. Not one of my fellow passengers matched the voice I'd just heard. I was *sure* I hadn't imagined it, but imaginary or not, the voice had made its point.

I looked out the window and watched the pine woods and the Cape Cod towns roll by as the bus carried me home from the Boston airport. *Disembodied voice plants seed of self knowledge*: it was about as woo-woo as you can get, but it was only the beginning. The door to the Other Side had just cracked open, and my long-dead mother was about to walk through it.

The funny thing is, I wasn't even trying to get in touch with Mom when, just a few days later, she sent me her first message from the Other Side. She'd already been gone four years, and while I missed her, I wasn't mired in grief or reading up on spirituality. To be honest, I wasn't really thinking about her at all just then.

As a university librarian with a Ph.D. in natural resources, I moved in a world that definitely did not take spirit communication seriously. Personally, I found reports of spirit contact interesting. I just didn't think they had anything to do with me. Turns out I was wrong.

That afternoon I sat outside pursuing my quest to become a human bird feeder. For more than a week I'd tried to tempt the wild chickadees into eating out of my hands. Each day I reduced the seeds on the bird feeder and inched my chair closer until at last I sat directly under the empty feeder, my cupped hands brimming with shelled sunflower seeds, the chickadees' favorite food. Two fat black-capped fellows perched above me eyeing the seeds I held out to them. They were so close I could count their little black toes clinging to the edge of the empty feeder and see their tiny black bills moving as they cocked their heads from side to side, eyeing the seeds and deciding whether to trust me. Overhead I could hear seagulls calling as they headed out toward the open water of the Atlantic Ocean and Nantucket Sound. An orange and brown towhee landed nearby, and leaves went flying into the air as she vigorously scratched the ground looking for whatever it is towhees find under all those layers.

I looked up into the trees and thought about the voice on the bus. Through the open window behind me, I could hear my husband, Frank, talking to the dogs and lighting his pipe. The familiar scent of his tobacco drifted out to me. It was true I wasn't entirely happy. Still, it was such a luxury to have an entire year in our own Cape Cod house, a cottage built by Frank and his father years before we met.

We'd driven five days across the country from Utah, three dogs in the back of the car, to spend a sabbatical leave here in the house we loved. With a year to work and write, we headed straight for Massachusetts and Cape Cod. We'd kept our noses to the grindstone through the cranberry harvests of fall, the winter snowstorms, and spring's tiny birds hatching in the dunes of our favorite beach. Now, in late May, those same little puffballs had grown real feathers, and when they ran ahead of me along the beach, their legs moved so fast they seemed to glide above the sand without touching the ground.

Cape Cod is alluring with its lighthouses, foggy mornings, quiet ponds, and crashing ocean beaches. Frank and I loved our home in the mountains of northern Utah, too, but arriving in Massachusetts and making our way down the Cape always felt like coming home. Even the familiar damp scent in the air brought waves of homecoming comfort each time we arrived and unlocked the cottage door.

Retiring to Cape Cod was a cherished dream, and year by year I'd worked to transform the summer cottage into a well-insulated year round sanctuary. I'd systematically replaced the skylights and appliances, ordered new windows, and installed new carpets and flooring in every room. I painted the furniture in bright cottage colors, with figures of seahorses and dancing mermaids. We hung oars and life preservers and lobster trap buoys from the rafters and turned the yard into one giant flowerbed of our favorite perennials. Suspended from the ceiling, a life-sized mermaid swam in the air above the dining table. I'd poured my heart into our beloved Cape Cod refuge.

But now, as I sat under the bird feeder listening to the calls of the chickadees, listening to Frank inside changing the CD player and opening the refrigerator, I acknowledged for the first time an awareness slowly seeping through the layers of my denial. My cherished dream of retiring to a seaside refuge, surrounded by love and wrapped in a cocoon of comfort, might already be lost. Twenty-three years of living with Frank's alcoholism and depression had taken their toll.

I suppose it was the night of Frank's third suicide attempt, just days earlier, that the realization finally sank in. I'd laid awake in bed that night, unable to sleep, listening to my husband stumble through the living room. After bumping around in the bathroom, he finally crashed to the floor, sprawled out in the hallway. A glance into the bathroom revealed that once again he'd consumed a cocktail of pills on top of an unknown quantity of alcohol. I dialed 9-1-1.

With Frank safely loaded into the ambulance, a policeman offered to drive me the twelve miles to the Hyannis hospital. I declined, saying that perhaps I'd just wait and drive over in the morning. When the policeman stared at me and blinked, I realized the whole suicide thing was getting a little old. I ended up following the ambulance to the hospital one more time. Trailing their tail lights through the dark, it dawned on me that if Frank died that night, my lack of hysterics might make me a murder suspect, but I was too numb to care. As terrible as depression is for the sufferer, it's every bit as devastating for those who love him.

My mind returned to the chickadees, and I glanced up at the feeder. Now there were *four* beautiful little birds cocking their heads and looking down at me. I held my breath. Suddenly three of them flashed away with a burst of wings, but the fourth brave fellow remained. He was so close I could see his eyes watching me, weighing the risk. The buffy color on his sides blended into the white below and contrasted with the gray above. He was beautiful. I focused and tried to send him thought waves of reassurance. Then, with one flit of his wings, he dropped so suddenly that I jumped. His tiny feet gripped my index finger. He snatched one, then two seeds, then three, and then he was gone, perched on a branch far over my head, enjoying his prize.

I was thrilled! I could still feel his tiny toes grasping my finger, his near weightlessness as he grabbed as many seeds as he could carry. The hours of sitting motionless day after day, inching my chair closer and willing him to trust me, had not been in vain. I was thrilled. Turns out my dearly departed mother was thrilled, too.

2

It was late when I switched on the desk lamp and scribbled "First chickadee lands!" on the calendar. I was puttering around the house, drying the dishes, gathering up the accumulated newspapers, folding the laundry, and feeling very much alone in spite of the three pairs of eyes following me from sink to table, into the guest room, and back again. Buddy, the big golden retriever, lay on the couch, chin on his paws and eyes drooping. Katie, the black lab wild child, had plopped down in the middle of the room and barely lifted her eyes as I stepped over her. But Jock, the ever-vigilant border collie—who stood up for all 2,600 miles from Utah to Massachusetts so he could snap at every passing car—was not content to watch me work. He followed me from room to room and back again.

I could hear Frank snoring softly in the bedroom. It was long past my bedtime, but a weird jittery feeling was keeping me awake. I felt like I'd drunk an entire pot of coffee. My whole insides vibrated with energy. As the night ticked on, I was exhausted but still wide awake. Finally every towel was folded and every coffee mug was put away. There was nothing left to do but go to bed and try to sleep. My whole being hummed with energy as I slipped into bed and took a few deep breaths in the dark. Even my hands tingled. Rolling onto my side, I called on my meager meditation skills to quiet my brain.

Suddenly an unexpected image flashed into my mind. It wasn't a dream; I was wide awake, but it clearly wasn't my own thought. Like telepathy, it came from outside myself. I saw a picture of me, a mental video of myself approaching, wearing blue jeans and a favorite raggedy gray sweatshirt, walking toward the "camera" of my mind. As I watched with fascination, I saw myself sit down cross-legged on the ground and place my hands, palms up, on my knees. In my palms were sunflower seeds, and chickadees instantly alighted and ate from my hands. My eyes flew open in the dark. No disembodied voice said, "This is your Mother speaking," but I knew it was. It just was. It was a message from my mother, who passed away from heart failure four years earlier. Mom's meaning was clear: "I'm still with you, and I'm very much aware of what's going on in your life." I'm pretty sure she added, "Good work with the chickadees!"

How did I know the message was from my mother? I don't know how. I just knew. Call it telepathy or infused knowledge or thought transference. I just *knew*, and the knowing was part of the message.

Grinning, I closed my eyes and took a few more deep breaths. In moments a new image appeared. This time I saw a procession of four *Peanuts* comic strip characters following each other across the screen of my mind. Suddenly, Peppermint Patty appeared in the upper right-hand corner of the picture. She opened a door, disappeared through it, and the door slammed shut behind her.

Again the meaning was clear to me. I'd been plodding along in a job that didn't feed my soul, feeling trapped in my post as a university librarian. In the scene played out in my mind's eye, I was the independent Peppermint Patty, and Mom was giving me a nudge to stop following the crowd and make a break for a more fulfilling job.

A third image appeared: pizzas, dozens of them, scrolling past from the bottom of the screen to the top. Aha! Clearly, Mom was telling me to quit my job and open a pizza parlor! Just two weeks earlier, I sat in my favorite hometown pizza parlor telling my friend Sally that I'd love to open my own pizza joint, and now Mom had spoken: "I am still with you. Quit your job. Open a pizza parlor." As I lay grinning into the dark, the hum of energy in my body subsided, and at last I slipped off to sleep.

When noisy blue jays woke me, the bedroom was already filled with brilliant morning light. The moment I opened my eyes, Mom's messages sprang back to my mind in crystal clear detail. I was enchanted with the knowledge that she had reached out to communicate with me from the Other Side. It never crossed my mind that I was dreaming or hallucinating or imagining it all. The knowing was just that clear.

As I listened to Frank's regular breathing beside me, I suddenly wondered whether I could request a message for him. I slowed my breathing, cleared my thoughts, and silently asked whoever was listening out there if there was another message. Just like the night before, my hands began to tingle with energy.

Then the entire "screen" of my mind lit up in bright pink. *Pink?* I thought. *Okay, it must be a reference to a female.* Next the screen turned to green, then alternated pink and green, pink and green. Okay, green for life, so a *living* female. Just like the night before, each image was accompanied by an instant understanding of its meaning.

Next, a single eye appeared, then an old fashioned key, and again the single eye. I understood: the single eye was the key. Frank's mother, Joyce, had recently lost the sight in her left eye. The message must be for Joyce, who lived just across the street.

Now the lower half of the screen was covered with tiny, multicolored dots. In my mind I said, *I don't know what that is.* No sooner was the thought sent out than a lobster plopped down into the scene. The dots were beach sand! Another confirmation that the message was for Joyce, a longtime Cape Codder.

Then came the roses. Pink roses, beautiful roses blossoming one out of another, over and over, and with the roses came the understanding that they symbolized love. Finally, a single pink rose that nearly filled the screen appeared—with a single eye in the center. Just like the night before, I telepathically understood the source of the message. It was a spectacular message of love from my father-in-law, Allan, who'd passed on more than a decade earlier.

I jumped out of bed and wrote down what I'd seen. Then I raced to the computer to research pizza franchises.

Poor Frank woke to me raving joyfully about quitting my university job and devoting our life savings to a pizza parlor. As if that weren't enough, I informed him that the instructions had been personally delivered by my mother, whom he knew for a fact had been dead these four years past. Frank took one look at me, announced "Not with my retirement money!" and went out for a drive, taking the dogs with him. I watched as he backed out of the driveway and drove away.

That hadn't exactly worked out the way I expected. In fact, Frank's response was so resoundingly negative that I wondered if perhaps I'd misinterpreted Mom's message. I sat down on the couch, re-envisioned the Peppermint Patty scene, and asked for clarification.

The telepathic connection kicked in immediately, and I quickly got my explanation. The four characters moving across the screen were the four remaining family members, while Peppermint Patty was my mother, ducking out a side door to heaven. And the scores of pizzas scrolling past? A symbol for my hometown and the family seat. Whenever I visit, I make time for a barbeque pizza at my favorite pizza parlor. I had to admit it was a better symbol for the town than, say, the county courthouse.

Looking back, I'm amazed how easily I accepted that Mom's very first message was actually coming from the Other Side. At best, a skeptic would say I was gullible, but the telepathic understanding that Mom was the sender was so strong, I never doubted it. I was thrilled to hear from Mom, but I had no idea how completely she had just changed my life.

3

I didn't *not* believe in communication from the Other Side before Mom contacted me. In fact, after watching television medium John Edward and his show *Crossing Over*, I wanted a reading of my own and had booked an appointment with a Boston-area medium, but that reading was two months away. Apparently Mom decided not to wait for the medium's help.

I was surprised to find that Frank wasn't a total skeptic about his dead father's message to his mom. In fact, Frank could remember Allan holding conversations with *his* deceased father whenever there was a difficult decision to be made. Joyce appreciated the news that Allan was sending her his love, and she, too, remembered Allan's conversations with his departed father. I just thought it was amazing to have received the messages, and I wasn't expecting any repeat performances.

It was late morning two days after Mom's messages, and we were waiting for the carpet cleaner to arrive. Frank took the dogs in the car for a ten-minute errand to the corner store and promised to be right back to pick me up. While the carpet dried we would drive down the Cape, grab some lunch, walk the dogs on the beach, and enjoy the beautiful day.

I sank into my favorite overstuffed chair and looked up into the beams of the great room while I waited. The light breeze wafting through the house was heavenly, and I idly wondered whether I would ever receive another spirit message. Then I wondered if I could *invite* another message. I laid my head back, took a deep breath, and cleared my mind. The image of a racehorse appeared, accompanied by the thought "Kentucky." Kentucky is where Frank and I met. The shape of Kentucky appeared behind the running horse. Now the horse disappeared, replaced by Frank's face, and I watched as Frank's glasses grew larger and larger until his face disappeared behind them. What was that supposed to mean? Next, an intense tingling began in my hands and feet, then I felt a terrible pain in the top and back of my head, and suddenly the meaning was clear to me. Vision problems (the enlarged glasses), tingling, and sudden headache: at this very moment, on the road and with three dogs in the car, Frank was suffering a stroke.

I jerked my head up and looked at the clock. He'd been gone twenty minutes on a ten-minute errand. The message was clear. I was certain of it. Frank was somewhere on the road, in an accident or in the ditch. I tried to calm down, telling myself it was too early to assume the worst, but my belief in the meaning of the message was complete. Just as when the first messages arrived, I was absolutely clear that it was a communication from the Other Side, and I was positive my interpretation was correct. I *knew* it. Frank was already dead!

I thought of borrowing his mother's car to drive out and look for him, but when I glanced across the street, her car was gone. I forced myself to wait until Frank had been gone thirty minutes before dialing the local police station. An officer who sounded about twelve years old told me, no, there had been no accidents involving white Jeeps with Utah license plates.

I considered the possibilities. Frank might be in another nearby town. Or perhaps he was depressed and with all the preparations for the carpet cleaner, I hadn't noticed. If that were the case, it was possible he'd driven out to some beach, parked the car, and simply swum into the waves until, exhausted, he drowned. He'd actually talked about committing suicide that way.

I was so sure of the message, so certain Frank was already dead, that my main concern was for the dogs, to be sure they weren't hurt, running loose, or losing their way in unfamiliar territory. I waited another fifteen long minutes and dialed the police again. How could I express the urgency of the situation, make them believe in the truth of a spirit message? Obviously I couldn't say, "Look, I'm a psychic, and ... ," or they'd send an officer after me instead of Frank.

I dialed. "I just have this intuition," I heard myself explaining. "I'm certain my husband is hurt." At least I didn't tell them he was dead, thereby making myself the prime suspect when his body was finally found. The same young officer assured me it was much too early for the police to get involved. "Could someone just check the parking lots at his two favorite beaches?" I asked. No, he told me, the officers have routes to patrol and can't be diverted from their assignments. I couldn't believe it. Not be diverted to look for a lost citizen in two specific locations? It would take me all of 15 minutes if I had a car myself.

I dialed the next town's police department. No wrecks there involving Jeeps from Utah. In all, I called five towns without success.

The carpet cleaner arrived, but by then I could hardly focus to talk to him. I took the phone out onto the front porch and sat down, trying to decide what to do next. Finally, I called the local police one more time, and the same young officer was so curt with me that I hung up on him just as my brother-in-law pulled up across the street. I dashed over and frantically asked him to drive me around to look for Frank, explaining that I'd had another spirit communication and I was certain he was in trouble. I didn't mention the part about Frank already being dead.

At that moment, a white Jeep with Utah plates pulled into our driveway with three dogs hanging their heads out the windows and Frank behind the wheel. He had been gone more than an hour on a ten-minute errand. Never in twenty-three years together was I so angry with Frank as the moment he pulled into that driveway alive and well. Mostly, of course, I was angry because the twelve-year-old policeman had been right, but the carpet cleaner was in the house, and there was nothing to do but get into the car with Frank and the dogs and go for a long, long drive.

You'd think I would have learned my lesson when I misinterpreted Mom's first communication and thought she was telling me to open a pizza parlor, but clearly I hadn't. Apparently the tingles I felt that morning were simply the physical sensation of spirit communication—a sensation I'd soon learn to recognize. And I suppose the images were simply spirit small talk. We met in Kentucky. Frank needed new glasses. And it turned out he had a severe headache that morning. Obviously, spirit communication was not one of my natural talents.

4

For the next few days I could hardly close my eyes without images and messages from Mom popping into my mind. There were signs naming and acknowledging various family members—cats for my brother Dave, golf tees for Dad, and a buffalo for Frank, who was born in Buffalo, New York. Sometimes the images were accompanied by a telepathic understanding of their meaning, like the picture of an elephant that arrived with the thought "don't forget" and the pink dogwood tree blossoming above a gravestone that came with the telepathic message, "I'm alive!" Other times the images arrived without translation, and it could be a challenge to decode them.

In one message Mom broke the news that a new baby was on the way. The message started with pictures of flying insects: flies, gnats, mosquitoes, one after another. I had no idea what she was trying to tell me. Then the Batman symbol appeared. Okay, bats eat flying insects. But why was she talking about bats?

Suddenly, in my mind, I saw a streak of light arrive from the upper right-hand corner. As the beam of light reached the center of my mental screen, it became a pulsing sphere of light. Telepathically I understood "baby" just as two tiny feet kicked out from the sphere and disappeared back into the glow. "Boy or girl?" I asked and laughed when the pulsing light turned a lovely shade of baby blue. But who was pregnant? And what on Earth did bats have to do with a baby?

The final image was a picture of false teeth clacking away, Mom's symbol for my brother Bob, who never wears his dentures. Could Bob and his wife be expecting another child? Maybe, but that still didn't explain the bats.

By the next day I still hadn't puzzled out the message. Frustrated, I sat down, cleared my mind, and demanded, *Okay, who's pregnant?*

The Batman symbol reappeared, and in my mind I heard Mom's somewhat exasperated reply, "*Casey* at the bat!" Sure enough, Bob's son Kasey was a father-to-be, and when the baby arrived, of course it was a boy.

Why didn't Mom show me a picture of a *baseball* bat? I haven't a clue, except that if she had, I probably would still be pondering, "Bat? Batter? Pitcher? Baseball? Ball park? Hot dogs?" Obviously she thought the combination of Bob and bats would lead me to Kasey, but then, I'm the one who thought she was telling me to open a pizza parlor.

The flow of spirit communication was amazing, delightful, and often funny. Mom had given me a whole new lease on life, an adventure that was all my own. I never questioned the source of the messages because the telepathic knowledge that they were from Mom was utterly clear and the accompanying sense of goodness was so strong. Later, I was surprised when friends and acquaintances sometimes asked if the arrival of the messages scared me. Never, not once, was there a single scary thing about them.

I loved the messages. They brought a sense of adventure and joy into my life, a brand new calling, but they were exhausting, too. At first they kept me awake all night as I alternated between receiving Mom's images and turning on the light to scribble down what I'd seen. Finally I moved into the guest room because I was keeping Frank awake. I was sleep-deprived myself.

The messages were fascinating. It was like playing charades, with Mom showing Dad's house number to indicate my father, a sailboat to say smooth sailing, a baseball diamond to signify a diamond ring and marriage, an open umbrella for protection. Other times a picture simply stood for what it was: a dog, a car, a mountain, a cigar. Often I understood a symbol from the context in which it occurred, and as symbols began to repeat, I got better and better at catching Mom's meaning. Pink referred to females, purple to spirits, red to love. Happily, the telepathic connection often accompanied the messages so I simply *understood* her meaning at the same time she showed me a picture.

Out of the blue one day I saw an image of our golden retriever, Buddy, followed by a picture of ocean waves. *True,* I thought, *Buddy loves water.* Then came a picture of Buddy standing chest-deep in the waves. At that point, I began to suspect the message was from Buddy himself, and he wanted to go for a swim. Next I saw another golden retriever's head, smaller and more delicate than Buddy's. As the view widened, I saw Buddy mounting the other dog! Apparently he wanted to go for a swim—and get laid.

Soon Mom began sending more serious messages. Inundated by images, I was wide awake at 2:30 one morning when an inviting country road appeared in my mind, curving away over a lush green hill and inviting me to follow. As I drifted along above the road, a wide, lush agricultural valley opened below me, dropping away to my left. Above the valley, but far below me, flew a pure white biplane.

My view panned from the valley up into a deep, dark, and starry sky, then down again into a sort of wide and starry bowl. My attention was drawn to a vast scene where many busy angels moved among large round tables. Telepathically I understood that I was seeing working angels, and that I would be working among them. That was a surprise. A lovely thought, but I couldn't imagine how it might come to pass.

The next day I was wiped out, completely exhausted from the messages arriving day and night. I loved it, but I really had to get some sleep. I went to bed early, cleared my mind, and addressed Mom and whomever else might be sending me so much information. I told them, *I can't possibly keep up with your energy. I'm sorry, but I* have *to sleep. In fact,* I added, *if you talk to me now, I won't listen.*

Our dog Katie was curled up next to the bed. I laid on my side and made a spot for her to jump up and cuddle with me, hoping that petting her would help me block out the spirit messages so I could sleep. I patted the bed and made kissy noises, but Katie could not be enticed to join me. She stood up and looked at the bed, whined, and retreated from the room.

It was a moment before I sensed why Katie had fled. An invisible someone was already sitting in the curve of my body, just where I had invited Katie to join me. I could feel a loving energy surrounding me and the physical touch of an arm draped lightly over my back. I literally felt the touch. *Mom!* I thought with joy.

Suddenly there was a second invisible presence in the room. A hand took mine, ever so gently, and held it while stroking my forearm. *This* spirit was definitely Mom, with her characteristic gesture of stroking the inside of your forearm to convey comfort and caring. As Mom held my hand and I felt the physical touch of our fingers closing around each other's, the first spirit leaned closer over me in a gesture replete with loving-kindness. Who could the first spirit be, sitting in the curve of my body as Mom held my hand? I didn't know, but the sense of being enveloped in a cocoon of their loving affection was otherworldly. I sobbed, both with the comfort they brought me and with the certain recognition of my mother, there in my room and very much alive, if not actually in the flesh.

Then I begged again for sleep. I told them, "Thank you *so* much. Now I'm going to go to sleep, okay?" But they weren't finished with me yet. Mom continued to hold my hand, and as she gently massaged it, both of my hands began to buzz, to hum with spirit energy. Without knowing how I knew, I understood that healing energy was flowing through my hands.

In my mind, a red and white lighthouse appeared through windswept trees. The beacon stood high on a promontory overlooking stormy, tossing waves—filled with whales! Everywhere I looked whales spouted and whale tails jutted out of the churning waves. Above the tumult I heard Mom's message,

"You get to be a lighthouse." Then she showed me a charming old vine-covered New England style house surrounded by trees and standing next to the lighthouse, and added, "But you get to live in a regular house."

5

That Memorial Day of 2003, when I received Mom's first message, wasn't actually the first time I'd heard from her since her passing four years earlier. She communicated with me the day she died.

Frank and I had arrived in Mexico anticipating our favorite kind of vacation with swimming, snorkeling, and scuba diving. I'd visited Mom and Dad just three weeks earlier, and I knew Mom would not be with us much longer, but I didn't comprehend how near her passing really was. Two days later the call came telling us Mom had passed away.

We walked out to the hotel beach, watched the waves, and let the news sink in. After a while, Frank went back to the room for our snorkels, and when he returned, he told me, "There's a red flower in the room." I looked at him stupidly, and he repeated, "There's a red flower in the room. It's on the counter by the sink."

Sure enough, there in a water glass next to the sink was a beautiful red carnation framed by two pathos leaves, a lovely makeshift floral gift. It seemed obvious to me that the flower was a gift from Mom, a sign of her love at the time of her passing when I was so far from my family. Did she magically cause the flower to appear out of thin air? No, there was a pin in the stem that told me it had been somebody's boutonniere, but there wasn't a doubt in my mind that she arranged for it to be placed in our room that day.

A few hours later, as I sat under a flowered beach umbrella watching the waves in the brilliant sunshine, I looked up to see a perfect white dove sail past overhead. The dove circled back, landed nearby, and stayed in sight around us all afternoon. Maybe it was just my grief, but the meaning seemed perfectly clear: another loving greeting from Mom, safely arrived on the Other Side.

By this time even Frank was beginning to see a spirit hand in the red flower in the room and the appearance of the white dove. That evening he found himself in the elevator with a man carrying a flower arrangement big enough to adorn the hotel's lobby. The man and his partner were departing after a week's stay, and the flowers had graced their room. When Frank mentioned that my mother just passed away, the man said, "Well then, these are for you!" and thrust the huge arrangement into Frank's arms. Chagrined, Frank arrived at our room with the massive bouquet and told me the story. "He said his name's Joe," Frank concluded, "but that was God, right?" Either God or Mom.

Earlier, while Mom was still very much alive, I received the first of three related spirit messages that arrived over a period of several years. After more than two decades of contact lens wear, my eyes had finally rebelled and rejected the contacts altogether, and I was considering laser surgery to correct my nearsightedness. The clinic I called informed me that my left eye was probably too nearsighted for correction, but scheduled me for a screening appointment in Salt Lake City, eighty miles away. Frank and I were just leaving for the appointment when his son Coll telephoned to ask if we'd seen the current issue of *The New Yorker* magazine. We hadn't. He would only tell us to get a copy and check out page thirty-three. Frank was anxious to find the magazine as soon as possible, certain that the mystery article would relate to Coll's work as a supervising sound editor for movies.

As soon as we arrived in Salt Lake, we tracked down a *New Yorker*, and sure enough, on page thirty-three was a major article about one of Coll's films. As we walked from the bookstore to our car, Frank handed the magazine to me. I flipped it open randomly and was taken aback to find a large cartoon in which a laser pointer had reduced someone's head to a wisp of smoke. It certainly looked like a bad omen for my laser surgery quest. Flipping to another random page, I was confronted with the bold headline, "When doctors make mistakes." Now I really had to wonder.

As we lunched at a small café, I had trouble focusing on the conversation. I couldn't get over the red flag that someone seemed to be waving in my face. I kept thinking about the whopping string of coincidences for Coll's phone call to catch us on our way out the door, for us to buy the magazine *before* my appointment, and for me to randomly open first to the anti-laser cartoon and then to the medical mistakes headline. Finally I looked at Frank and said, "You know, I'm really kind of getting the idea God doesn't want me to have this surgery."

Frank's eyes met mine. "I think you're right," he said. That was all I needed to hear. I picked up the phone and cancelled my appointment. When the cheerful receptionist asked whether I'd like to reschedule, I declined, but I left out the part about God telling me not to do it.

I never knew why I was warned away from laser eye surgery, so when I received an advertising flyer from a different vision company three years later, I looked it over. The cost of the surgery had dropped dramatically since my first inquiry, and when I called for information, I found out the technology had progressed far beyond the correction I needed. *Maybe,* I thought, *instead of "Don't," the first message really just meant "Wait."* I made an appointment for a screening consultation.

The day before my new appointment, Coll telephoned to ask if we'd seen a recent *Time* magazine that reviewed another of his movies. As I flipped through the library's stack of past issues, I came to one that featured a dramatic cover story about laser eye surgery. *Good timing,* I thought, as I perused the well-balanced article presenting pros and cons of the procedure.

The article closed with some questions to ask your doctor before surgery. A sidebar listed an acceptable complication rate to compare to your own doctor's record while another item cited research indicating that a physician's complication rate drops dramatically after performing 300 laser surgeries and again after 600 procedures. I picked up the phone and dialed the clinic. When I asked for the doctor's complication rate, I was told, "Oh, we don't have that information."

"Can you at least tell me how many of these surgeries he's performed?" I asked.

To my astonishment, the young man replied, "We've asked him, but he won't give us that figure." He hesitated, then added helpfully, "But I *can* tell you it's more than fifty."

Suddenly I recognized the perfect replay of my first eye surgery warning three years earlier. The screening appointment is made—Coll telephones—look for a particular magazine issue—movie review—laser eye surgery warning. Surely this was no coincidence.

Don't get me wrong. I'm not suggesting laser eye surgery is an inherently bad or dangerous procedure. I can only tell you that for *me* it's inadvisable, though I may never know exactly why. After the second warning I promised never to consider eye surgery again. When God tells you something once, that's one thing, but when *God* tells you *twice*, it's probably a good idea to listen. Even after two warnings, though, I still wistfully read all the advertisements for laser vision correction—not that I had any intention of doing anything about it other than polishing my perfectly functional eyeglasses.

A year later, during our sabbatical on Cape Cod, the local paper regularly carried advertisements for eye clinics in Toronto, where laser eye surgery was a fraction of the U. S. cost. When Boston-to-Toronto airfares plummeted, I remarked to Frank that at current rates, a person could fly to Toronto, get the eye surgery, fly back for the one-week follow-up exam, and return again for the one-month check-up all for less than the cost of the surgery stateside. Not that I intended to do it. From the Other Side, Mom put her foot down.

Three days after receiving her very first image of chickadees eating from my hands, Mom sent me a picture of eyes, lots of eyes looking right, looking left, up, down, and straight ahead. The next image was of eyeglasses, pulsating and growing larger and larger until they filled the screen. Now the eyes reappeared, each with a beam of light touching the eyeball—clearly a reference to laser vision surgery. Eyeballs and laser beams filled the screen. In the midst of all the eyeballs, a small, neat red X appeared. I sent out the thought, *If you're trying to tell me not to get surgery, you really ought to make a bigger X than that.*

Instantly—KABOOM!!!—a giant red X filled the screen, blotting out all the eyeballs and laser beams. I finally got the message: "Never, but never, get eye surgery. And stop asking!"

6

O n the seventh day of Mom's messages—at 4:30 a.m.—she gave me an assignment. I suddenly found myself wide awake in bed, eyes still closed, knowing that another message was on the way. Both hands were humming with energy. As I waited, I felt a pain in my left knee, then another pain in the second toe of my left foot, and thought, *Maybe these are places Dad has pain from his World War II injuries.*

Talk about woo-woo. I felt pain and seemingly out of the blue thought, *I wonder if this is where Dad has pain from his war wounds?* I didn't even know Dad still *had* pain from sixty years ago. The only way I could possibly have made that leap was by telepathy. The information didn't even match what I knew of my father's World War II wounds. Since childhood I'd known that one of his *big* toes was messed up in the war. If I were guessing which toe still gave him pain, I would never have guessed the second toe of his left foot.

Suddenly both of my hands began to buzz intensely, and a new telepathic message came through loud and clear: I was supposed to lay hands on Dad's war wounds to relieve his pain. My response was instantaneous: "No way! Not gonna happen." Me "lay hands on" my father? Absolutely not. Our family is very reserved, yet very emotional. We keep our emotions in check on a massive scale, and such a loving ministration would be more than either of us could bear. And how could I explain Mom's assignment to him without sounding like a nut case? It didn't take any thought at all to know that this was a very bad idea, but as I drifted back to sleep, I heard a line from the movie *Field of Dreams:* "Ease his pain."

Sometime later I was awakened by a sharp pain in my right wrist. It had bothered me off and on for weeks, and I'd been wearing an elastic support for it. At the same time, my hands began buzzing again, and I took the hint that I was supposed to lay hands on my own wrist. I placed the palm of my left hand squarely over the pain. In my mind's eye I saw streams of white light flowing not into my painful wrist, but into the hand covering it. In a matter of seconds the pain vanished, and my wrist felt better for the first time in weeks.

I couldn't deny that the energy directed through my hands in the wee hours of the morning had a healing effect on my wrist. Mom was making her point, but I still wasn't keen on telling Dad that Mom, from the Other Side, was directing me to lay hands on his war wounds. The next night I cleared my mind and prayed the most fervent prayer of my life, asking for confirmation of her message. "I'd better not be making this up!" I whispered into the darkness. As I drifted toward sleep, I heard the movie words again: "Ease his pain."

It was still dark when I woke again, this time with the feeling that I was being sent upstairs to the guest room to "take a message" without disturbing Frank. Ensconced in the guest bed, my left knee and the second toe of my left foot began to hurt again, and in moments my hands were positively zinging with the sensation of healing energy. Moving my hands through the darkness, I could feel the energy rolling off them in waves. "All right!" I snapped, "I'll do it." Then I asked the all-important question: "Precisely HOW do I do this healing thing with this energy in my hands?"

The next idea that popped into my head was the actor Ned Beatty. Ned Beatty? What on Earth was that supposed to mean? I hadn't thought of him in years. An image of Ned Beatty and Ellen Barkin in their roles from the movie *The Big Easy* appeared, and then I laughed. Mom was telling me it would be simple. I asked, "How am I supposed to do this healing thing?" and she answered, "Big easy!"

Soon I saw an image of Dad lying on his bed while I placed my hands on his knee, his shin, his foot. It did look easy. Now if she would only tell me how to break the news to Dad. I'm sure it was no coincidence that at the time of Mom's first instruction to do healing work for my father, I already had a plane ticket to visit him just three days later. It took three days for me to agree to do it.

Dad met me at the Indianapolis airport, and as we drove north, I told him about the messages I'd been getting from Mom. I talked about the symbols and images and described some of her jokes. I told him how Mom had even sent pictures of the big-nosed Kilroy cartoon, kidding Dad from the Other Side about his Alm family nose, just as she had in life. Dad listened and agreed that it was all fascinating. I've never been so thankful for Dad's generous and uncritical nature.

I didn't mention healing until my brother Dave joined us that night for barbeque pizza. I recited some of my favorite anecdotes again, then slipped in the zinger. "But that's not the interesting part," I said. "Mom wants me to lay hands on Dad's war wounds and stop the pain. And furthermore," I told them, "she even indicated where the pain is." I described the sensation of pain in my knee and in the second toe of my left foot, then looked at Dad. "Is that right—at all?" I asked doubtfully and was dumbfounded when he replied, "That is *exactly* right."

I was stunned. This was an extraordinary confirmation for me because I simply hadn't believed that particular toe could be a problem. It was the very first external validation of my psychic abilities, and it had a huge impact, reassuring me that I really, really wasn't making it all up.

The next day I mentioned the healing to Dad again and asked if he thought we should do it. Bless him, he replied, "Well, I think that if you're supposed to do it, then you should do it." Then he joked, "Besides, it might help my golf game." Turns out he wasn't entirely kidding. The pain was sporadic, except when he played golf. On the golf course, the pain was always with him.

We decided to put Mom's instructions into action on Sunday, since that seemed like the proper day for spiritual undertakings. Mom kept prodding as the day approached. I suppose she thought we'd chicken out. One day a staff member at my brother Dave's computer store was doodling a jaunty tune in his booming bass voice when he suddenly stopped to announce, "I'll bet nobody knows what that tune is!" Nobody knew. "It's Ned Beatty's theme from the original *Superman* movie!" I couldn't believe my ears. Ned Beatty again? What were the chances? Then, while driving around on various errands, Dad and I ran across—get this—a lighthouse! It was a great big replica of a lighthouse standing at the front of a modular home sales lot. I'd never seen it before, but there it was, right there in landlocked corn belt Indiana. Mom was reminding me of her promise, "You get to be a lighthouse."

When I woke up on Sunday, my hands were already humming. After breakfast, we attended Dad's Methodist church, and as I listened to the service and gazed into the beams above, I pondered our upcoming experiment in healing and asked God for His blessing and His help. Suddenly a thought popped into my mind that I *know* I didn't put there. The thought said, "Invite the minister to be present for the healing."

No way! I thought back. *Absolutely not. N-O, no. I have no idea what I'm doing, and I'll be darned if I'm going to have a minister there to watch me make a fool of myself. Don't do this to me!*

Then the voice calmly added, "At 2:00."

I couldn't believe it. I leaned over to Dad, whispered to him about the new message, and asked what he thought. He shrugged and said, "I guess if you're supposed to. But don't be surprised if the minister can't come. It's awfully short notice, and his schedule is really busy."

Relieved, I turned my attention to the sermon in time to hear Pastor Craig speaking of physical healing and how physical healing can lead to emotional and spiritual healing. He spoke of physical healing as a sign of God's activity in the world, and I realized that inviting Pastor Craig might be as much for him as it was for us. I rolled my eyes heavenward and thought, *You win, Mom. We'll ask him.* To Dad's amazement, the minister agreed to join us. Dad was amazed; I was not thrilled. The worst news was that, at the moment, Dad was pain-free. Still, since we'd been told to invite the minister, we were apparently supposed to proceed.

After church Dad and I went out for lunch and then wound our way home by a circuitous route due to road closures. To my surprise, yet another lighthouse appeared, this one standing at the entryway to a housing development. Mom was making sure I didn't back out.

When Pastor Craig joined us, we chatted a bit about my new experiences, and he offered some wise insights, pointing out that God's healing does not always arrive in sudden and miraculous forms. The results of today's endeavor might develop over time. In some cases the result of a healing ritual might be to seek further help from the medical establishment. Finally, with diplomacy so incredibly kind and subtle that I nearly missed his meaning, Pastor Craig suggested that he hoped I didn't think my healing talents came from within myself. When I realized what he'd just said, I assured him I had absolutely no delusion that any such healing power was my own.

We adjourned to the bedroom where Dad removed his shoes, pulled up his pants leg, and stretched out on the bed just as Mom had shown me. Pastor Craig offered a prayer thanking God for His healing gifts, for life after death, and for communication beyond the grave. I waited for the buzzing in my hands to escalate, then gently placed my hands on Dad's knee.

I felt like an idiot. I could feel the energy humming in my hands, but I had absolutely no idea what I was doing. I moved my hands a bit lower on Dad's leg and was struck by the softness of his skin. What was I supposed to be doing while I inched my palms along Dad's shin? Praying intently? Sending powerful thought energy to the source of his pain? Picturing him pain free, skipping through fields of daisies? What was I doing here, claiming to have some healing power, some direction from beyond, performing some serious ritual in the presence of my trusting father and his *minister*, for God's sake?

When I reached Dad's foot and gently placed my hands on either side of his toes, I stopped. I didn't know what else to do, so I looked at Dad and the minister and said, "I guess that's it." Dad gave me a hug. Pastor Craig thanked us for including him and bid us goodbye. Mingled with the hum of energy, I could still feel the touch of Dad's soft skin on my hands. Later, as we said good night, I told Dad, "Well, I hope it helps. And thanks to Mom."

He added, "Yes, and thanks to the Source."

The next day I noticed the church newsletter on the dining room table. The logo at the top was a lighthouse.

I took a shuttle bus back to the Indianapolis airport. As I leaned my forehead against the cool glass of the window, I wondered how many other fathers would have believed my crazy story. I wouldn't have believed it myself.

I was lucky to be born to such remarkable parents. My two brothers and I grew up in a loving and supportive household that nurtured creativity and self confidence. Mom and Dad were both schoolteachers, and I admired them for their dedication and their devotion to their students. They were incredible role models— kind, caring, giving, and nonjudgmental.

My upbringing was solid and comfortable, Midwestern, middle class, and protestant Lutheran. My parents were serious about their religion without being fanatical and nurtured extended family relationships so we never felt alone in the world. They cared about others, supported charities for the homeless and hungry, and worked hard to help out when anyone was in need. Now, when *I* needed it most, with my marriage failing, Mom was there helping me, opening the door to a whole new life. Returning to my university work seemed insignificant compared to the opportunity and excitement of exploring my newfound spirit connections. As the airport shuttle bus rumbled along I could feel the energy still humming in my hands.

With my hands buzzing and my tired head bumping against the bus window, I gazed up into a sky filled with puffy little clouds and was delighted to see cotton candy colors. It was lovely—pink in one cloud, blue in another, and green in the next. As we rolled along the highway, the colors changed, blending from turquoise to bright green to sunny yellow. I was enchanted and assumed the magical effect had to do with the angle of the light coming through the bus windows. Glancing around me, I was amazed that no one else was looking out the window and enjoying the light show in the clouds. Tired as I was, I couldn't close my eyes on the delightful view, and I resolved to watch until the direction of the bus caused the colors to disappear. The funny thing is, even as the road curved in a new direction, the colors remained.

7

I was too early to tell whether Dad's pain was gone for good, but I was hopeful, and the energy in my hands stayed with me. Sometimes it was a throbbing pulse and sometimes a tiny hum, but it was always there. I discovered that I could banish my own headaches simply by placing a hand on my forehead. I wondered if this gift would remain, what conditions it would heal, whether I could use it to help other people, and how I could find out. Who would ever let me practice on them? When Frank complained of a headache, I offered to place my hands on his head, but he never took me up on it.

By now it was June on Cape Cod, and our house was full of company, but I made a little time every day to sit outside with the birds and reflect on what might be ahead, woo-woo-wise. The idea of leaving Frank had been percolating for a long time, but I felt I had nothing in the wings to leave him *for*, nothing to move on to. From the Other Side Mom had changed all that. For the first time in years I glimpsed a future full of fascinating possibilities. On the other hand, maybe Mom's whole purpose for getting in touch was to stop Dad's pain, and now that I'd completed her assignment, the healing energy would depart and the messages would stop coming. So far, though, she was still communicating.

I didn't have a regular beautician on Cape Cod, so when I walked into Rose's shop one day for a haircut, we'd never met. I liked her immediately, and we had a great visit as she clipped away and I admired the family photos that decorated her counter top. When Rose pointed out the picture of a son who'd died in a car accident, Mom butted into my thoughts, informing me that I could bring Rose a message from her son. I was thrilled that, far from cutting off our connection, Mom wanted to teach me even more spiritual skills, but I was not thrilled with the idea of informing a woman I'd only just met that my dead mother was telling me I could bring her a message from her dead son. I said nothing, paid my bill, and left.

It took more than a week of continuing nudges from Mom before I went back to Rose's shop and explained that I might be able to bring through a message for her. To my relief she turned out to be a fan of television's *Crossing Over with John Edward*, so she knew all about mediumship, and we set a date for my first attempt to receive a spirit message for another person.

First, however, I had to figure out *how* to do a reading for another person, and Frank's mom agreed to be my guinea pig. As we sat in Joyce's living room, I closed my eyes and cleared my mind. It took only a few moments before pictures and symbols began to arrive. First came the initial A. For Allan, Joyce's late husband? Then a bicycle appeared. It was a tandem bike, trailing a long woman's skirt. Did Joyce know what that might mean? She knew exactly what it meant. On their first trip to Bermuda years ago, Allan and Joyce had great fun on a rented tandem bicycle. I was delighted. Right off the bat Allan had identified himself by sending a picture that was meaningless to me but represented a strong and loving memory to Joyce.

It turned out to be a wonderful reading. Allan sent image after image that had meaning for Joyce, including a diamond ring (marriage), pink and red roses (love), trains, and airplanes (they were world travelers). Then he sent an image that looked like a knight in the game of chess. It took me a moment to realize the picture was actually the horse head emblem on the front of Prince Valiant's tunic in the Sunday comics. So my mom wasn't the only spirit who poked fun from the Other Side. Joyce had never been allowed to forget the time she threw out Frank's and his dad's collection of *Prince Valiant* comic strips in a moment of cleaning frenzy.

Then, in a fascinating sequence of symbols, Allan identified one family member after another. First came the silhouette of a baseball pitcher, suggesting Joyce's father who pitched for the St. Louis Browns in the early 1900's. Next he showed me the baby cradle made by his own father. Now a bird, a robin, an obvious reference to his son-in-law, Robin. Two hungry baby birds in a nest with mouths wide open suggested Frank and his sister. Then came a picture of the tarot card called "the hanged man." Looking it up on the internet later, I read that the hanged man card represents spiritual awakening. Allan was acknowledging me! He had identified in turn both grandfathers, his children, and their spouses.

As it turned out, the hairdresser Rose and I never connected for her reading, even after scheduling and rescheduling. I guess her role in my spiritual growth was to help me think beyond messages from my mother alone, and for that I'm grateful to her.

Just a few days later I had a chance to practice my mediumship again, this time with my long time friend Kathryn, a Boston schoolteacher. In back-to-back readings both her Great Aunt Maria and her Grandma Vee came through. Alarmingly, both sent warning messages, presumably related to Kathryn's upcoming trip to Guatemala with a medical mission.

The first message came from Great Aunt Maria. Following the first letters of her name, a pointer to her homeland of southwest Italy, and images of her famous perfectly round sugar cookies, I suddenly got a telepathic "NO" combined with a picture of a roulette wheel. It was a strong "Don't gamble" statement. The reading continued with identifiers for various family members, including a sequence I couldn't decode: the letter K, a baby carriage, another K, then a butterfly. I was stumped, but Kathryn laughed and said, "That's easy. Mom and I are both named Kathryn, and she has a butterfly-shaped heart valve. K-butterfly is Mom. K-baby carriage is me."

Next, Grandma Vee came through loud and clear, identifying herself with the letter V followed by a grandmotherly nightcap like the ones pictured in children's books of Little Red Riding Hood. She acknowledged family members, identifying each of her children with a symbolic image. Like Great Aunt Maria, she used a butterfly to indicate Kathryn's mom, then she showed me a model airplane to denote her two sons who've been flying model planes for years. There was one picture, though, that had us both stumped. It was a big male walrus with long ivory tusks. A walrus didn't ring a bell for either one of us. When I asked Grandma Vee for clarification, the tusks just got larger. I wracked my brain and finally threw up my hands, saying, "I just see a great big walrus with *huge* ivory tusks."

"Oh, that's Aunt Patty!" Kathryn laughed. "It's the ivory! She was a concert pianist and still has a room full of pianos in her house." Apparently Grandma Vee was trying to get me to say the word "ivory." I have no idea why she didn't just show me a piano!

When Grandma Vee proceeded with *her* warning message, it was much more strident than Great Aunt Maria's roulette wheel. First she showed me a Santa Fe Railroad diesel engine, then the shape of Texas. Unknown to me, Kathryn's Guatemalan trip would begin with visits to friends in both Santa Fe and Texas. Then Vee sent an image of a frog lying helpless on its back, his pale belly exposed. A spiny, crab-like creature was reaching out with pinchers to attack the defenseless frog. I was shocked by the image and its implication of vulnerability and imminent danger. I described what Vee was showing me and made Kathryn promise their group would take extra safety precautions during the trip. To this day, that remains the only frightening image I've received in any spirit communication. I don't mind telling you I was relieved when Kathryn and her medical colleagues returned safe and sound from their mission to Guatemala.

The best part of mediumship is bringing through information that I couldn't possibly have made up or guessed, and I quickly learned to start every reading by asking the spirit to send an identifier that will clearly communicate their identity. A middle-aged woman named Mattie Ann hoped to hear from her brother Easton. When he promptly sent me an image of a rabbit, Mattie Ann laughed so hard she could only nod in recognition. One Easter when they were children, their father sent them large chocolate figures from Los Angeles. Easton promptly ate his, but Mattie Ann proudly displayed her chocolate rabbit on the dining room sideboard for days. When she finally succumbed to temptation, she carefully lifted down her bunny only to discover that *someone* had nibbled away the entire back side of it.

When a young mother named Shelly came for a reading, her Uncle Harvey sent one identifier after another including a preference for Chevy cars, a Chevy convertible, and a horse. But he really knocked my socks off when I heard the words "totem pole" and Shelly laughed, saying, "Oh, yeah, they had a totem pole in their front yard."

In a reading for a young woman named Debora, her friend Betty showed me a can of tuna, and her pal Dar sent me an image of pink bedroom slippers. Debora grinned because these were the two things she always teased them about. Betty insisted on making tuna salad without draining the oil from the fish, and Dar always wore fuzzy pink slippers with her sexy dressing gown.

My friend Peggy called me shortly after her brother-in-law Jack committed suicide. Her husband and son were in Alaska cleaning out his house. Jack came through loud and clear saying, "Be careful of my pipes." When Peggy called her son that night, he told her Uncle Jack's tobacco pipes were everywhere. That very afternoon he'd accidently stepped on one!

Lying in bed one night, I sent out a thought to Mom, thanking her for the fascinating and wonderful changes she had brought into my life. Her gifts infused my life with new meaning and gave me something exciting to work for. Then I told her how much I missed her. I told her how I wished she were here in the flesh right now so we could give each other a real life hug. A picture of two ends of rope wrapped around each other appeared in my mind. At first I thought it was Mom's way of telling me she was still here with me, that we were together, then suddenly I recognized her meaning. She was sending me a visual hug, exactly what I'd asked for.

A moment later I saw an amusement park ride with teacup-shaped cars spinning at dizzying speed. I saw myself clinging to the lip of one of the teacups, my body flapping in the breeze as the ride whipped around in twirling circles. In my mind I heard Mom's amused prediction, "Hang on for a wild ride!"

8

The summer was filled with visiting friends and family. Cape Cod's lakes and ocean made entertaining grandkids and nephews a breeze. When we could get them out of the water, we went whale watching and seal watching, ate fresh seafood, picnicked on the beach, and drove out to the tip of the Cape, to the wild and woolly artists' colony of Provincetown. Life was busy and happy, but I still lived with the insecurity of never knowing when Frank might be drinking, and the joy of my recent woo-woo experiences only highlighted my discomfort.

I put my spiritual explorations on hold as my emotions seesawed, summer activities swirled around us, and I attended to all the preparations for the drive back to Utah. I sometimes went days without a message from the Other Side, but there was one wonderful moment of external confirmation that let me know I was in no danger of losing my spirit connections.

Months earlier—even before Mom started sending her messages—I'd scheduled a telephone reading with a Boston area medium. The appointment finally arrived just two days before we departed for home.

I was impressed when she accurately described some of the formative events in Mom's background, but when she said, "There's something about healing in your life," my jaw dropped. With that simple statement she confirmed everything for me— Mom's contact, the healing, the rightness of pursuing these mystical developments, and a whole new direction in my life.

Through the medium, Mom observed that there was conflict with Frank at the moment. No kidding. All the new developments were difficult for him to accept, and I'm sure he was wondering where it all would lead. Mom said that healing—mental, intellectual, and emotional—was being sent to Frank from the Other Side. I was impressed with the reading, except for one thing. When Mom said, "Within a year you will be buying and selling real estate," it sounded impossible. There was no way we would be selling either the Cape Cod house or our home in Utah.

Frank was interested in what the psychic had to say, but when I told him I'd made an appointment for a second professional reading the next day—by a "transitional seer" from Santa Fe who was staying with an acquaintance nearby—he was furious. Just hours after my inspiring reading, Frank faced me across the living room coffee table and gave me an ultimatum. I was going to have to make up my mind, he said, whether I was going to live in this world or some other world. If I was going to live in some other world, he told me, he didn't think he could live with me. He would be forced to divorce me.

I had an eerie sensation of utter calm as I listened to his anger and frustration. Over the last few weeks he'd vacillated between supportive and desperately uncomfortable, and I could understand his anxiety. Surely I'd feel the same in his position, but I knew in my bones that I was already past the point of no return. I had been chosen, and I had accepted the gift. There was no going back.

The next morning I went to the second reading, but I didn't get much out of it. My mind was reeling with the realization that divorce was imminent. Returning home, I stood in the front yard surrounded by the brilliant reds, yellows, pinks, and purples of my flowerbeds. I would miss them all. Then a dash of new color caught my eye. In every flowerbed, a few stalks of tiny blue flowers nodded among the lilies, delphiniums, and hollyhocks. Forget-me-nots, a flower we'd never planted, suddenly seemed to peek out everywhere. Forget-me-nots! It had to be another gift from Mom.

I spent the afternoon packing into the car everything in the house that was mine alone—clothing, books, and keepsakes. I knew then that I wouldn't be back.

9

We drove west toward Utah and home with our belongings on top of the car and three dogs in the back. Besides time for research and writing, a sabbatical leave provides an opportunity to step back and reevaluate your direction and your priorities. It's a time to think and a chance to move in new directions. In my case, "new directions" was putting it mildly.

We stopped over for a few days with Dad in Indiana, where Frank got drunk in a restaurant, only reconfirming that it was time for me to go my own way. That night Mom sent me an image of a cornucopia spilling out a bountiful harvest. With the cornucopia came her reassurance: "Good will come from divorce."

Our next stop was a sobering reminder of what I stood to lose in a divorce. Visiting Frank's daughter, Anna, and her family in Omaha, we swam and picnicked and laughed together as I wondered what my future family life would look like. Would the stepchildren and grandchildren I loved be lost to me?

We stopped in our favorite Omaha bookstore, and for the first time in my life I found myself drawn to the New Age section where one title jumped out at me: *Whose Hands are These?* by Gene Egidio. I knew before I pulled it from the shelf that it was about laying on hands healing and that it had been sent to me, or rather, I had been sent to it. As I held Egidio's book in my hands, a second title jumped out at me: *Opening to Channel* by Sanaya Roman and Duane Packer. I'd heard of channeling, allowing a spirit to use your voice to communicate, and it didn't seem that different from mediumship. I paid and tucked the two books under my arm, confident they were a gift from the Other Side.

On the final day of our journey west, as we wound our way down through the last beautiful mountain canyon that led toward home, Frank raised the possibility of divorce. I looked out the side window at the steep cliffs and the spectacular river that plunged along, following the highway, and thought of all the conversations we'd shared as we planned and dreamed together on Sunday afternoon drives up this same rugged canyon. How many times had we snaked up the canyon highway and down again, taking in the beauty of mountains and sky as we hammered out our stresses at work and our vision for the future? Should we have a child of our own? Should we apply for that job? Should we sell the Cape Cod house? Were the kids okay? The parents? The dogs?

Frank was still talking. Perhaps we might want to separate for a bit, he suggested, and get a feel for what our options were. As I listened to him throwing out ideas, I knew that my decision was already made. "Actually," I said as gently as I could, "I really do need a divorce. I'm sorry." It seemed to take Frank by surprise. Though we'd occasionally talked about the possibility of divorce, I realized he had no idea I'd already reached a decision. Had he somehow not noticed that I'd packed all my personal belongings into the car with us?

Arriving home, the dogs bounded happily through the house and raced out into the yard, happy to be home. I carried one armload after another from the car to the house, making space for everything in corners and on counter tops until the unpacking and the laundry and the re-settling-in would begin. Wandering through the house we'd left a year earlier was unsettling. The house was so familiar, yet it felt distant. Our lives there were so familiar, but suddenly nothing was the same. It was a strange sensation, strange partly because without yelling or recrimination our paths had suddenly diverged. Amicable. It was as amicable as a divorce could be. As darkness fell, exhaustion and familiarity exerted themselves, and we fell into bed together and slept.

The next day Frank suggested that we give the marriage one more year to pay off debts and enable him to stay in the house rather than be forced to move to an apartment. It was a foregone conclusion that he would get the Cape Cod house and I would keep the house in Utah. He promised to give me every opportunity to develop my spiritual work. I jumped at the straw of hope he was offering, then moments later declined, knowing that I really did need to move on. Only later did I realize that he hadn't actually said anything about not divorcing. In his mind, too, our marriage was over.

It was strange how simply such a momentous decision seemed finally to have been made. Just like that, I lost everything I'd loved and built my life on, and just like that, I gained the opportunity for a fresh start. I felt the call to be a healer as clearly as if Mom were there in person encouraging me. I'd move back to Indiana for the first time in thirty-two years and be near my family. I would throw myself completely into my new calling and give myself a year to establish a healing practice.

Later, as I sat soaking in the bathtub, it dawned on me that if I was moving to Indiana, there was no reason for me to get the Utah house in the divorce settlement, only to turn around and sell it to a stranger. And if Frank kept both houses, he was going to need two houses' worth of furniture to fill them. So it was agreed: Frank would keep everything except my personal belongings and would buy me out with a monetary settlement. It would make my move that much easier.

The only complication was that after a sabbatical leave, the university requires you to stay on at least a year, so my new life was on hold until the contract year ended the following May. It would be months before I could pursue my plans for a healing practice, and it would be months before our financial settlement was finalized and I had cash in hand to move on with my life.

In the meantime, I needed a place to stay. A friend of a friend had a condo for rent, and I set out hopefully to see it, but when I stepped across the threshold of the tiny apartment, I was greeted with dark gray living room walls and a minuscule kitchen made even smaller by walls painted midnight blue. Not a stick of furniture was included. When the young woman told me what they were asking for rent, I burst into tears and never even made it upstairs to see what nightmare colors they'd painted the two tiny bedrooms. I arrived home in tears, and Frank came to my rescue, assuring me that I could stay in the house with him until I moved to Indiana.

Even as we met with one lawyer and then two, Frank and I continued to share the house, three dogs, and a bed. The lawyers wrote into the divorce settlement that I was allowed to stay in the house until May if need be, and I was grateful to Frank for that concession because renting a decent furnished apartment in a college town was obviously out of my price range, and I had no intention of asking for alimony.

In a matter of days Frank was striking up friendships with new women. He bought flowers and prepared a gourmet meal for our former house cleaner. He was in touch with a mutual friend we'd often invited to visit us, and she e-mailed, encouraging me to pursue my new calling. He went home with a woman he met in a bookstore, or maybe it was a video store. The day I came home from work to find him sitting on the hearth with a tall blonde in short shorts and his bare foot resting on the inside of her thigh, I turned around and walked back out the door. I drove straight to the furniture store, purchased a twin bed for my home office, moved it in, and closed the door behind me. Remarkably, there was no anger. We each had what we wanted.

Two of the dogs seemed oblivious to the change in our relationship, but Jock, the border collie, attached himself to me, following me from room to room. At least somebody was looking after me. Jock was going to be a Hoosier.

10

It was liberating to begin establishing my own routines for a whole new life. The first Saturday home I got up bright and early to check out the local gardeners' market. Everyone said how wonderful it was, and everyone was right. It was a lively mix of produce and craft vendors with food booths and live music, coffee, and fresh squeezed lemonade. Everywhere I turned I was greeted by friends who welcomed me back into town. I stopped for a seated massage, and the therapist's relaxing touch unleashed the tears I'd been holding back. I felt alive at the market and realized for the first time how zombie-like I'd been for the last few months. Everything about the market was fresh and fun.

Halfway back to the car, hands full of peaches and tomatoes, I had an inspiration. If massage therapists could have booths and work on clients at the market, why couldn't I have a booth to do my healing work? The organizers scratched their heads for a moment, then agreed that they didn't see why not. It was another gift, a chance to practice, to develop my healing skills while I waited for the opportunity to work at healing full time.

At home I deliberated how to present myself at the market. Simply coming right out and announcing I was on a mission from God didn't seem like the right way to go, but that was essentially what I did. I made two signs and put them in frames, created a short flyer explaining how my deceased mother got me started and my father was my first patient, picked out a cheery tablecloth, and bought two folding chairs.

On Saturday morning I arrived at the market a half hour before it opened. I set up my table, spread out the bright red and white checked tablecloth, and set up the signs I'd made: "Healing Hands FREE" and "Spiritual healing for people and pets." I sat down beside my table, took a deep breath, surveyed the milling crowd, and wondered who in the heck would be crazy enough to let me work on them.

To my amazement, I soon had my first taker, a woman who had a headache and neck pain. I don't remember if my ministrations helped her, but I remember my next patient very well. A white-haired and blue-eyed retiree named Sandra lowered herself slowly into my client chair, her hips and knees aching with arthritis pain. I placed my hands gently on one knee, then the other, then behind each hip in turn. I could feel the healing energy humming in my hands. Sandra felt tremendous heat penetrating her aching joints, even though my hands remained cool to the touch. The intensity of the heat surprised even me, and when I finished, I was embarrassed to see that the warmth of the energy from my hands had literally ironed a crease into the knee of Sandra's white slacks. She's told me many times since that for weeks afterward her pain was simply gone, and later, if twinges of soreness returned, the discomfort vanished when she reflected on that first healing experience, holding in her mind's eye a vision of my hands on her knees.

My next taker had a headache brought on by eating dairy products. As I laid my hands on her head and sent out a silent request for healing energy to help her, she said, "I can feel things moving around in there." In minutes her headache vanished.

Of the seven people I worked on that first morning, several promised to report back on whether it had helped, four commented on the sensation of warmth from my hands, one felt an inner coolness, two said they'd be back next week for another treatment, and one left a message of thanks on my answering machine the following day.

As soon as I "hung out my shingle," non-traditional healers seemed to come out of the woodwork. Almost every market day I was approached by rapid eye therapists, ear candlers, dream therapists, Reiki masters, reflexologists, muscle testers, colon hydro-therapists, iridologists, craniosacral massage therapists, and a woman who claimed she could realign my DNA. At first I was delighted to find I wasn't the only woo-woo in the valley, but as I listened to their claims, it was clear that most of them were full of baloney. But then, who was I to criticize? Why did energy flowing through my hands make any more sense than realigning DNA? In other people's minds, I was sure to be lumped in with the wackos. It was a sobering thought.

I had come out of the closet with my new calling, though it was another week before I heard myself claim the role and simply tell people, "I'm a healer." My new mission in life was launched, *I* knew it was genuine, and I was thrilled. I had something real to offer, a gift that would benefit others. So what if I had to work in the library for nine more months? So what if I was getting a divorce? For the first time in my life I had a real calling.

Almost everyone I worked on commented on the heat from the healing energy, but soon people were reporting more surprising sensations. Some told me they felt movement, tingling, or a hum moving through their bodies. Many reported the arrival of a profound sense of peace and well-being. More than one person fell asleep in the chair as I worked on them, and a woman named Kennita reported that as I held each of her hands between mine, there in the midst of the busy market crowd, she was transported to a place of utter calm as if she were back in the womb.

On my fourth Saturday at the gardeners' market, with fewer than two dozen healing sessions under my belt, a spirit came to call. A dark-haired woman named Kristine said that a friend sent her to the market to see me. I was delighted—until she told me her son had taken his own life just two weeks earlier. I couldn't begin to imagine the pain she must be feeling, and I wasn't sure I could help her.

I'd read you could send healing energy throughout the body by placing a hand on the back of the neck, and I'd added this simple action to my healing routine. This simple touch almost universally produced a deep and calming sense of well-being as I placed my other hand at the small of the client's back, on their forehead, on their crown, or on their chest. This was all I knew to do for the grieving woman now seated before me. As Kristine leaned back, closed her eyes, and slowed her breathing, I placed one hand behind her neck, the other on her chest, and directed my loving thoughts to her, saying a prayer for God's support in her great loss.

Minutes later, as I moved my hand from her chest to her forehead, she whispered, "I saw a white light." It was a brilliant white and glittering light, she told me. At first she thought her eyes were letting in some daylight, and she squeezed them closed. Then, in the midst of the beautiful light, a pink childlike figure came and stood before her. When the light and the child disappeared, she squeezed her eyes tighter, hoping to see them again, but the vision was gone.

Neither of us knew what to say. I wondered if it was a visitation from her son, but I doubted he would represent himself in pink. Perhaps it was an angel, a spirit, a "being of light"? We simply didn't know, but clearly it was meant to bring her comfort. It was a gift to both of us, a comfort to her and another confirmation to me that what I was doing was real and heaven-sent.

11

As I described my new experiences to curious strangers at the gardeners' market each week, I gradually developed a short version that evidently didn't sound like I was a total nut case because every Saturday new people let me work on their aches and pains, and some returned again and again.

It was much harder to explain myself to friends and coworkers who had known me for years. Sometimes I invited old friends to be my guinea pigs, offering to work on a headache or an earache or do a reading for them. It didn't help that a few years earlier my friend Mary Jo had given me a book on palm reading and I'd read scores of palms while admonishing everyone not to take my palm reading any more seriously than a fortune cookie. Now I was enthusing, "Forget the palm reading! This is *real*."

More than once Mom whispered to me, "Don't forget to heal animals!" so when my friend Susan invited me to try my healing energy on their dog Trigger, a 12-year-old German short hair, I jumped at the opportunity. Trigger had suffered a dislocated shoulder years before, and combined with the effects of age and an intolerance for arthritis medication, he was quite lame on all four legs. Trigger was a sweetheart, and he appreciated every bit of my attention as I laid my hands on his shoulders and hips and then worked my way down his spine.

When I saw Susan the next morning, she reported that Trigger was still very uncomfortable, but he was more chipper than they'd seen him in months. A few weeks later she e-mailed me, saying, "Trigger has taken to once again jumping on the bed to greet us in the mornings. He runs up and down the stairs, and he accompanies me on two-to-five-mile walks several times a week. We took him pheasant hunting for the first time in several years, and he found and retrieved birds for us. He's an old dog, but he's an energetic, enthusiastic, content, and good-natured dog." I was amazed. You couldn't get *me* to go on a five mile walk!

Other friends let me practice doing readings for them. Julie, a forty-something mother of teenagers who seemingly never stops laughing, is my oldest friend in Utah. Just a couple of weeks after our return from sabbatical, she and one of her daughters sat down with me for a reading. I warned them that I hadn't been receiving many messages lately and I was still pretty strung out emotionally over the divorce. I wasn't sure any spirits would be able to get through my mental fog.

I closed my eyes and slowed my breathing. A capital T appeared, followed by a miner's hat with a shining light mounted on the top. Julie and her daughter nodded. A grandfather with the initial T had been a miner. I closed my eyes again and watched as a story unfolded on the screen of my mind, and it wasn't just a few cryptic images. It was a full-blown, full-color movie in my mind, complete with physical sensations.

A small mining car descended on a track from my right and rolled to a stop before me. I thought, *He's sending pictures of miners' tools. He's reconfirming his job.* I kept my mind's eye on the little car, waiting for the next installment. Suddenly the mining car tipped over, rolling toward me and landing with its wheels spinning in the air. Before I could begin to guess the meaning, an avalanche of debris—rock and timbers—crashed down the tunnel route by which the mining car had arrived, smashing it against a rock wall to my left. As I gasped in surprise, a second avalanche of debris crashed down a previously-unseen tunnel chute straight ahead of me and piled the mountain of rock and timbers even higher. I felt the ground under my feet drop a few inches. Then silence.

Naively, I waited for a rescue party to appear down one of the tunnels now packed with debris. Finally I heard something—faint voices and digging far above and behind me, over my right shoulder. And that was all.

The stunning display of spirit communication left me with tears streaming down my cheeks and all three of us speechless, but the message was unmistakable: "It's me. I crossed over that day, but I'm still with you." Their grandfather died in a mine collapse.

Not every message was stunning, or even meaningful. A few were downright unintelligible. When this happened, the message typically was preceded by an intense jittery feeling. It was like the jitters I felt the night of Mom's very first message—times ten.

One evening as I felt the ultra-jitters coming on, I closed my eyes and saw an image of a mother cradling an infant in her arms, gazing on the child with profound love. The glow above their heads told me it was a picture of Mary and the baby Jesus. Small, childlike angels wearing colorful dresses appeared in the air above Mary's head. A dove appeared. One cherub rang a bell, another blew a trumpet, a third played a hammered dulcimer suspended by a strap around her neck, and yet another played a French horn. Angels were celebrating the birth of the holy child, but even as I watched the message unfold, I thought, *That's nice, but duh! Some spirit's going to a lot of trouble to tell me angels were happy when Jesus was born?*

The super-jitters continued, and another message began. There was a peace symbol, then the same symbol upside-down. *Peace, then no peace?* Next I saw the prow of a battleship, bristling with guns. An aircraft carrier appeared, followed by images of military tanks and more tanks and still more tanks. Images of war kept coming as the message dragged on for more than half an hour.

Sad faces appeared, one after another, with frowns and closed eyes. Then an upside-down sad face followed by more and more sad, motionless, upside-down faces. The hair of the women spread across the ground around them, and it was clear they were dead. A cherub peeked down soberly from above and scanned the deathly stillness. An angel with wide-spreading wings appeared. Everything below remained silent with death and destruction.

Soon I saw a circle, divided vertically in half, one white side and the other side black. I understood that the white side of the circle represented the "haves," the privileged people who are not touched by war. The message rambled on.

Now I was shown a diamond necklace. The necklace was followed by fancy high-heeled shoes and spangled dresses. A glass of champagne. I saw the back of a curvy female figure wearing the skimpiest of bikinis. Then one small, sad face appeared and was quickly obscured by another bikini top, holding back bulging breasts. *Where is this message going?* I wondered. *As if I don't know that war is bad and hurts the poor, that innocent people suffer while the privileged party on.*

Now a sequence of letters and numbers appeared. I jotted them down as they came: F - E - 5 - 4 - 5 - E - 4 - 5 - 5 - 4 - K. Then a Z, an A, a Y. It rambled on, making no sense, but showing no sign of stopping. Finally, I called a halt. I simply tuned out, realizing that some unknown, but obviously less-evolved, spirit was taking advantage of my new openness to hold my attention and babble long and insignificant messages.

For the next week, each time I felt that super-jittery feeling begin, I closed my eyes and pictured a gray, shadowy spirit who wanted to talk through me. Over and over in my mind I drew the curlicue editing mark that means "delete" as I repeated, "I am not taking your message. Go to the light." The intruder came again and again, sometimes several times in one day, but he was easy to recognize by the jitters he caused, his inability to adjust his energy to mine. Each time he appeared, I was able to send him on his way with more and more forgiving thoughts.

Late one afternoon the intruder made his appearance as I wrestled with a project at work. I closed my office door, sat down and took deep, calming breaths, and placed my hands over my stomach. As I felt the warmth of healing energy flowing from my hands, I spoke to the spirit in sympathy, blessing him and encouraging him to go to the light. When I closed my eyes, he showed me a picture of a handgun, so I simply opened my eyes until the image of the gun went away. No need for negativity. I told him to go to the light, where he would find comfort and love. In my mind I showed him two spirits, full of light and love, who were coming out to meet him, and at last he began to move slowly in their direction. The heavenly spirits gathered him in as the intruder collapsed into their arms. They lowered him to the ground, enfolding him with warmth and comfort and sleep—and their wings. The jitters-times-ten were gone for good.

Meanwhile, new and positive experiences just kept coming. The first leaves were beginning to change color as I headed for work one September morning, radio on, mindlessly following the same route I'd driven for years. Suddenly something I can only describe as a huge wave of "Lonely!" hit me from the right. The feeling-message was so powerful that I did a U-turn and drove back to find the source. In an overgrown lot between two houses, exactly where the message had come from, stood an elderly dappled white mare, all alone. When I pulled over and walked up to the fence, she came to me immediately, so I stroked her face and promised to come back and visit her again. After work she was even happier to see me arrive with apples in hand, and from then on, I kept a bag of apples in the car just for her.

One day, as I stroked her face, I cleared my mind and waited, curious to see if the white horse would send me another message. The image that materialized in my mind reminded me of a toilet with the seat up. It looked like a circle with two vertical objects sticking up from the sides. I looked around for anything that resembled what she was showing me, but no luck. At work I asked a horse-savvy friend what the shape might be, but she had no idea. The next day I stopped again and asked the horse for clarification, but the picture she sent remained the same.

As I stood at the old picket fence of her yard a few days later, stroking her neck and wishing I knew what she was trying to tell me, my eyes fell on the gate in the fence, and there it was. The picket fence was held closed by a metal ring dropped over two of the slats: a circle with two vertical pieces sticking up. My friend was asking me to open her gate! I felt terrible because I obviously couldn't do that for her, but I could visit her and bring her apples. When the weather grew colder, the white horse disappeared from her lot. Wherever she was moved, I only hope that there are other horses so she won't be lonely anymore.

12

When Frank flew back to Cape Cod in October to visit his mother, it was the opportunity I'd been waiting for. One of the books I'd purchased on our way home from sabbatical, *Opening to Channel* by Sanaya Roman and Duane Packer, had convinced me that learning to channel was the next lesson in my own personal woo-woo school. As a channel, you allow a spirit to speak through you, using your voice to communicate, which makes you the spirit's channel of communication. I was already receiving messages from Mom and others on the Other Side. If I could receive messages in the form of pictures and telepathy, why not words? What I needed was time alone to practice, and Frank's trip provided it.

By this time, I was so confident of the reality of my own spirit communications, I didn't bat an eye when the book's introduction informed me that the book was written by Sanaya and Duane *and the two spirit guides they channel*. Their guides, Orin and DaBen, explained that many high guides are available and eager to work with human channels at this time, and I hoped one of them would work with me. The guides' goals, they said, are to increase human understanding of the spiritual realm, to assist us in making a positive difference in the world, and to advance the process of mankind's evolution.

I pored through the book and worked my way through the exercises on learning to focus, relax, and make contact with entities I couldn't see. Sometimes I wondered if I'd rounded the bend and turned into a genuinely crazy person, but remembering the unbelievable things I'd already experienced, I figured it wouldn't hurt to see what happened.

In one exercise, I held a fresh-picked daisy from the flowerbed, cleared my mind, gazed into the yellow depths, and waited for the daisy to send me a thought. The only thought that popped into my mind was, "Thank goodness Frank's not here to see this." I put the daisy aside and tried again, this time waiting for a large quartz crystal to speak to me. I placed the crystal in a patch of sunlight on the dining room table, cleared my mind, and gazed into the sparkling depths. A beautifully clear, chunky quartz point, it stood more than two inches high and was almost as large in diameter. In the depths floated a scattering of imperfections that looked like snowflakes captured in glass. I lost myself in the beauty of the crystal, and suddenly it *did* speak to me. In my mind, I clearly heard the words, "The imperfections don't matter." I was shocked, but I suppose if you already believe you can hear from dead people, a crystal shouldn't be an impossible leap.

Following the book's instructions, I prepared to meet my guide. I closed my eyes, relaxed, and focused my mind. I visualized moving up into the heavens and recognized that I was surrounded by loving spirits who welcomed me to their realm. Just as the book had said, I saw a large door before me and understood that by stepping through this door, I would confirm my desire to meet and work with a spirit guide. I stepped over the threshold and saw before me a semicircle of many spirits waiting to bring their loving support and guidance to our human experience. Before I could even voice my request for a guide, I saw her step out from the throng of spirits and move toward me with arms outstretched. She was tall and slender with long blond hair and wore a pale blue gown that reached the floor. Her approach and her outstretched arms communicated great love. We didn't speak, but I felt her love and acceptance enfold me, and we stood together without speaking. When it was time to go, I didn't want to turn my back on her, so I backed away, saying goodbye and stepping backwards through the doorway by which I had come.

When I opened my eyes and found myself at my own dining room table, my mind was reeling. What I had experienced felt so real and yet so un-Earthly that I leapt up from the table and began washing the dishes that were in the sink. I felt compelled to do something grounding, something concrete and Earthly, but I was grinning from ear to ear. I had met a spirit guide who loved me and wanted to work with me for the benefit of mankind and my own spiritual advancement. I laughed out loud as the sink filled with soap suds.

The next step was to establish verbal contact and find out my guide's name. I sat down with the book's list of suggested questions and cleared my mind. I pictured the guide who had greeted me, and asked for her name. No response. I tried a question from the list, "What is my life purpose?" Nothing. I waited, wondering exactly how something that was not my own thought was supposed to come out of my mouth. Then she was there. She appeared to me and embraced me as I sat on the couch hoping to hear her words emerge from my own mouth. I could feel her arms around me, but no words came. I took a break and tried again. Again my guide appeared and embraced me, but no words came to my mouth or to my mind.

Discouraged, I scanned back through the book, where an anecdote caught my eye. It described a woman who was unable to bring through a message from her guide until the spirit Orin instructed her to *pretend* she was channeling. I tried again and asked my guide for her name. The letter E appeared in my mind, followed by an I, and then an A. "I think your name is Eia," I said aloud, pronouncing it EYE-uh. In my mind I heard the reply, "Eia is correct." Contact! I abandoned the list of suggested questions and asked Eia what she would tell Ellen, a friend who was facing a terrible divorce. The answer came in pictures instead of words, but it came. Eia showed me a story of Ellen walking away from her difficult marriage and setting herself free. My very own guide was communicating with me, even if it wasn't yet verbal.

Recalling the woman who broke through by pretending to channel, I posed another question, "What is the meaning of my relationship with Frank?" Then I simply opened my mouth and began to speak, pretending to answer my own question. It felt exactly as if I were speaking my own words until I said something surprising: my years with Frank provided the opportunity to demonstrate that I am capable of living for someone other than myself. *That* was a new idea, and when I heard it, I knew it hadn't come from me. I started talking again, and Eia's words continued, telling me that I would pursue my hands-on healing, but that my main undertaking would be channeling her as she counsels people about their lives and their paths. And that, she added, is another kind of healing.

The next day I tried to contact Eia again, and this time the response was immediate. I asked her about a dog I'd done healing work for. Baby, a beautiful and sweet black cockapoo, had been run over by a car, and her back legs were paralyzed. She was unable to control her bladder or her bowels, and she moved by dragging her back legs across the ground. Baby's owner told me that when the weather grew colder, she would have to put Baby to sleep. My healing work did not seem to have helped.

I had no trouble speaking Eia's words as she told me not to worry about Baby. "Baby is a happy spirit," she said, "whose path is to be here with this family. She is here to help them learn to love. They *like* Baby, but they don't know how to love her."

"Are they learning anything from Baby?" I asked, and Eia said no, but they will have more opportunities to learn to love, and they will remember Baby.

"What will happen to Baby?" I asked.

"Don't worry about Baby," Eia told me. "She will go back into spirit where she will not have to worry about her Earthly body. She is fine now, and she will be fine then."

Then I asked a question that had been on my mind for weeks. I asked about the woman named Kristine at the gardeners' market, whose son had committed suicide. I wanted to know about the pink childlike figure that came and stood in front of her in the glittering light. "What was it that Kristine saw at the market that day?" I asked.

The perfection of Eia's answer stunned me. She said, "That was a spirit who has come to help Kristine find ways to help children."

13

B ack in July Mom announced, "Within a year you will be buying and selling real estate." It made no sense at the time, but here it was December, and here I was sitting at Dad's kitchen table in Indiana, combing the real estate ads. I couldn't leave Utah until my contract ended in May, but I could lay the groundwork for my new life as a healer.

For months I looked forward to moving closer to my family, but now that I was here house hunting, nothing was falling into place. Not a single house for sale seemed to meet my needs for living space and a healing office. I was so convinced of my calling that I couldn't believe the perfect house hadn't materialized, but after three weeks of fruitless searching, I admitted that maybe—like the pizza parlor—I'd once again misinterpreted my spirit communicators. I conceded that walking away from a full time university job might not be the wisest course of action, and I headed back to Utah to house hunt all over again.

Finding a house in Utah wasn't much easier. For more than two months I scoured the valley for an affordable house that would accommodate me, my dog Jock, and the healing work I still felt I was being called to do. Finally, worn down and completely stressed out, I gave up and turned the search over to God, the universe, or whoever was out there.

"All right!" I announced. "I give up. I leave it to you, universe, to bring me the perfect house." I ticked off my list of requirements: a town that would grant me a business license, a relatively new house, a nice yard for Jock, a garage, mountain views, trees, a healing room, an office, and a fireplace, all on one level to accommodate client access, and all within my modest price range.

The next day Dad arrived for a visit and encouraged me to reconsider the "for sale by owner" listings in the newspaper. We chose five listings, visited them all, and the fifth house was it. It was *the* house I'd been searching for. It was the first day the house was listed in the newspaper, we were the first people to look at it, and the owners accepted my offer on the spot. The universe had delivered!

Where Frank's and my house was isolated and surrounded by fields, my new home was surrounded by welcoming neighbors and swarms of kids. The block was full of bicycles and lawn mowers and trampolines. When I got over the shock of all the activity, it was like a breath of fresh air to be surrounded by so much life.

On my own for the first time in twenty-three years, my single living skills were a bit rusty. I accidently poured the oil into the gas tank of my brand new lawn mower, and I never did get the hang of using the weed trimmer, but I mow, I stain the deck myself, I recycle and put out my own garbage, and I catch my own spiders and dump them outdoors. I dig out the overgrown sprinkler heads in the spring, and I shovel my own driveway in the wintertime.

I love my little town with mountains in every direction and horses grazing in old barn lots on almost every street. I've looked out my windows at night to see deer nibbling my flowerbeds and wild peacocks walking up the middle of the street. I drive to the post office past sheep and llamas, goats and cattle, and even a flock of wild turkeys. Pheasants and baby ducklings cross the road in front of my car, and meadow larks sing from every direction. My deck is lined with bird feeders where siskins, doves, finches, flickers, red-wing blackbirds, hummingbirds, and grosbeaks call and the occasional kestrel sends them scattering in every direction.

I can hear chickadees in the neighborhood, but my trees are neither big enough nor close enough to bring them to my feeder. The pine trees I planted should provide enough cover for them in about sixty years or so. In the meantime, the stars of my feeders are flocks of little goldfinches. They show up every winter morning, and by the time they head north in April, their plumage has turned to brilliant yellow. All sitting in the neighbors' leafless aspen trees, they look like dazzling yellow Christmas ornaments.

Surrounded by snowcapped mountains, with roosters crowing and deer in the yard, Jock Dog and I had come home.

14

When Jock and I moved into the new house, our spirit friends were already there waiting to welcome us. Not that they hang around all the time, but they never fail to respond when I send my thoughts their way. Often they show up unexpectedly, and I know they're there when I get the sensation of someone lightly holding onto my wrist or my fingertips. I sometimes feel it while I'm driving, or in the middle of a conversation, or lying in bed at night. I usually don't know who it is holding my hand from the Other Side, but sometimes I can make a good guess. When my widowed friend Kay and I watched a play starring her daughter, I felt that spirit-hand-holding sensation, and it seemed pretty likely that Kay's husband had come along to watch his daughter perform.

At home, when I focused and contacted my spirit supporters, they told me that Eia is my primary guide, with me since my birth and orchestrating the arrival of other spirit helpers as their services are required. It never occurred to me to ask Eia about herself until friends kept asking who she was. Was she my grandmother? A ghost? An angel? Eia told me she's lived just two lifetimes on Earth, both "during the Middle Ages." In her first Earth incarnation, she said, she was a rabbi, and in the second, a priest. "The religious connection makes sense," I told her, "but a rabbi and a priest would both be males."

"Well you know, dear," she replied gently, "in spirit we have no gender. Those lifetimes gave me the opportunity to accomplish specific goals, but most of my work is done from spirit. I represent myself to you as female because it is appropriate to our work together."

When I perceived a male spirit sending me information during my healing work, his tall, thin build, black clothing, and top hat reminded me of Abraham Lincoln. I greeted him, and he introduced himself as Dr. Nu, saying, "I am already helping you with your healing work, and I welcome you to our higher realms."

"Should I channel your words for clients while I'm working on them?" I asked.

"You may channel my words if you wish," he said, "but it's not necessary. *You* will hear me and feel my instructions."

I was curious about his name. "Is it spelled N-U?" I asked.

"Yes," he responded, "but you may spell it N-E-W if you prefer." Curious, I consulted the internet and discovered that the Greek letter *nu* is used in physics and astronomy to designate a measure of the frequency of light. I'm no physicist, but I do appreciate that his name is linked to light and energy.

I asked Dr. Nu if my Abraham Lincoln impression of him was correct. "In actuality," he told me, "I am energy without a body. My appearance is only a convenience and a greeting."

When I inquired about his medical specialty, Dr. Nu told me that, unlike Eia, he has never had an Earth incarnation—and therefore no human medical career or specialty. He uses the title "Dr.," he explained, so that my clients and I will understand the nature of his work with me. When I do healing work, I often appeal to him to boost the energy passing through my hands and direct it to all the places it is needed.

Oddly, though he identifies himself with healing, Dr. Nu, like Eia, rarely gives specific medical advice and never provides diagnoses. Sometimes he'll make an observation like, "The pain does not originate solely in her knee. Her ankle is also part of the problem." If he says, "Trust your doctors" or "Don't neglect to take your thyroid medication," I pass along whatever I hear, but I receive so little specific medical or diagnostic information that I sometimes suspect I may be blocking it out. Perhaps, subconsciously, I just don't want the responsibility of conveying medical information.

Gradually I began to sense a second healing spirit assisting me. I glimpsed him only once, and he looked like a football player with a crew cut. He never spoke, so I called him "Dr. Hands" because it felt as if his hands were gently encircling my wrists as I worked.

As I did more and more readings, receiving messages from people who have passed on, I started to hear the name Roger during almost every session, but nobody ever claimed him. "You don't know anyone on the Other Side named Roger?" I asked one client after another.

Finally I appealed for Eia's help, and she told me it was about time I recognized that he was there for me, not for one of my clients! Roger, she said, is a spirit helper who assists in making connections with the Other Side. He assembles the appropriate spirits before each reading and makes sure they come through in an orderly fashion without overwhelming me. He asks the spirits to show themselves in clothing that represents their lifestyle and time period, and he helps them communicate their relationship to the person I'm reading. As Eia spoke, I saw an image of Roger reaching out toward me and backwards to those on the Other Side, forming a bridge for communication.

That explained Roger, but soon I was hearing "Williams" during every reading. Again, no one claimed him, so I asked Eia who this was. He turned out to be the spirit I'd been calling Dr. Hands, and he works in concert with Dr. Nu and Roger. According to Eia, he delivers an even higher healing energy than Dr. Nu's, and together they've been supporting my healing work from the start. Williams, Eia told me, is interested in developing all of my "spiritual aspects and attributes."

Once I knew who Williams was, I asked for him by name and easily made a connection. During our very first conversation, he politely read me the riot act. He said I must focus more when I do readings and promised to help maintain the vital energy connection that facilitates communication as long as I don't break my focus.

Other spirits occasionally make their presence known, and of course there's Mom. In a "movie" without words, Mom showed me her work on the Other Side. She's teaching school, just as she did in life, only this time she has just five children in her care. I watched two students using what looked like an extremely advanced computer, scanning through index screens in comic strip format at a tremendous rate. I saw a special needs student, too, receiving lots of loving one-on-one care and attention. As we walked together down the hall to a student-led musical activity, I felt Mom's pride in her new school, and I felt the love flowing among the students and the teachers.

Months later my friend Peggy, a medium and channel who never knew my mother, contacted Mom one afternoon while we were practicing our mediumship together. Peggy observed that Mom isn't around me as much as she was when she first started sending me messages. I knew that was true, and when I asked why not, Peggy said, "She's busy."

"What's she doing?" I asked.

"She's got a job. She's teaching children, little children."

"I knew that!" I exclaimed. "She showed me that! She was a teacher in life."

"Well, she's so proud of you," Peggy continued, "and she says for once you listened. She's really happy because she didn't think she'd be able to connect with you. She says that when they told her to make a connection, she told everybody, 'No, it will never work.' So she just did her best, and she really felt good that you finally listened."

Through Peggy, I asked Mom about her job on the Other Side, and she told me, "I'm teaching. I teach little children. It's different than my teaching in my Earthly existence, but there are all kinds of people who need to learn, and these are spirit children. I have five right now, and their names are Cheryle, David, Cynthia, Stephen, and Ashley." Five students—just as I'd seen in the vision she sent me.

"What do you teach them?" I asked.

"Oh, all kinds of things," Mom said. "Things like music and poetry. And like using your creative skills. I teach them manners, too." I had to laugh at the idea that spirit children needed to be taught manners, but the idea of Mom teaching creative skills made perfect sense. Developing creativity was one of Mom's great interests during her Earthly teaching career.

When I inquired what there is to do on the Other Side, Mom told me, "There are lots of things we do. There are schools, and there are universities—sort of like universities. And there are reincarnations, too. We could move on to another life. Or I might be somebody's guide for awhile. But my spirit can always be with you, no matter where I am otherwise."

When I asked whether she's with other relatives, Mom said, "People are scattered, and they aren't people. They're their spirit essences, and they go different places. We're not really people as you remember me being a person. I'm the essence of my spirit. And the family here is big. There is much more interconnection than our Earthly group that we would call family. Family has kind of a different definition. Everybody's busy doing other things, and some have reincarnated, and they live on. You'd never understand it anyway, but that's okay." Then she added, "It's a *big* place."

"If I think of you and say hello to you," I asked, "is that actually sort of disruptive to whatever you're doing?"

Mom laughed and said, "Oh, of course not. Thank you for thinking of me. Think of me as often as you want. Write me notes. Put the notes in a safe place, though, or they might carry you off to the booby hatch!

"I'm always here," she continued. "Don't miss me. I'm just as close as your call. I'm not *that* busy. I'm here, and I love you."

15

Any fears I might have had about becoming a lonely divorcee vanished in the freedom and exhilaration—and peace—of having my life back. Now I was truly free to pursue my new calling, and after a newspaper article about my work appeared in the local paper, even more clients began to make appointments for healing work. I still set up my table at the gardeners' market on Saturday mornings, but for the first time I had a real healing practice at home.

Fourteen-year-old Natalie, tall and beautiful with long blond hair, was one of my first clients in my new healing room. For three months she'd suffered unexplained daily fainting spells, and the doctors were stumped. Natalie lay on my healing table, and my hands smoothed her T-shirt as they moved lightly down her spine. I could feel heat and energy buzzing like crazy in my palms. As I shifted my hands to the top of her head, I glanced up at her mother sitting an arm's length away in the room's low light. Our eyes met, and we exchanged hopeful smiles.

When I finished, it was impossible to tell whether the energy had helped, but I knew Natalie had a good feeling about the session when she asked if I could treat her horse for nervousness. The next afternoon I stood beside Thumper with Natalie holding his bridle and my hands resting lightly on the side of his neck. The young horse took a small step sideways, then another, then another as he shifted away from my touch. "He may be feeling something from my hands," I told Natalie. "People often feel heat or a tingling sensation when I do healing work."

"Oh, I know," Natalie said. "When you worked on me, I saw a golden light." She stopped a moment, then added, "Or rather, I *felt* a golden light." I was amazed. It reminded me of the pink spirit child that appeared to Kristine at the gardeners' market.

When I saw Natalie's mom, Sue, at the market two weeks later, I was delighted to hear that Natalie's blackouts had not returned, and I told her Natalie's story of the golden light. "Oh, I saw it, too," she told me. "While you were working on Nat, there was a golden light in the palms of your hands." Now I was more than amazed; I was thrilled. *I* wanted to see the healing light in my hands, but it would be more than three years before that happened.

It was early January, and I was staying in Dad's guest room for a visit. One night I laid awake for what seemed like hours, my brain whirling with thoughts. Rolling over onto my side, I saw a blue-white flash and thought it was a beam from the streetlight hitting the latch on my suitcase nearby. Then I realized the window shade was tightly closed, and no outside light was entering the room. My left hand extended out over the edge of the bed before me, and as I looked into the darkness and wondered what I had seen, a brilliant blue-white squiggle of light appeared in the palm of my hand. It looked like a shining mass of tangled and glowing threads slowly rotating in space. As I watched, it slowly moved, still rotating, from my palm down my forearm, then disappeared. As soon as it disappeared, another brilliant blue-white tangle took its place in my palm, rotating and moving down my arm. I looked at the back of my hand, and another tangle of light appeared, moved down my arm, and vanished before it reached my elbow. Turning my hand over, there it was in my palm again. In all, the light appeared and disappeared six or seven times, then it was gone. I held out my other hand and looked at it in the darkness, but the light show was over. I never told anyone about the light. You just had to be there. It was way too woo-woo to explain.

Though no one else mentioned seeing light in my hands, almost everyone I worked on reported some sensation of the healing energy. The most common feeling was a penetrating warmth, though my hands remained cool to the touch. The more clients I worked on, the more surprising sensations they described. Some told me they felt buzzing, tingling, or movement, pulling or popping, "things opening up," or "energy moving." When I worked on my friend Mary Ann's old knee injuries, she laughed and laughed because the muscles of her knee and calf literally twitched. More than once a client's eyes flew open as they looked to see how I could have three hands working on them at once—a sensation somehow created by the energy. A man who saw drifting puffy blue clouds as I worked on him had a sensation of expanding beyond his normal body and becoming bigger than life. As the strange sensation slowly receded, it was replaced with a tingling, then disappeared altogether. Another client grabbed the edge of the healing table when she felt as if she were floating right up into the air.

Time and again people told me that their stress melted away with the arrival of the healing energy. Some not only fell asleep, but actually snored while I worked on them.

Best of all, some told me they saw light—turquoise or green or brilliant white and gold, pulsing light, enveloping light, rivulets of light, clouds of light, light shows with glowing shapes and shooting sparks, flashes and explosions of color, and light that looked like it was flowing up from a well. The light shows seemed to me to be especially emblematic of the healing energy's heavenly source.

One young mother brought her eleven-year-old daughter along when she came for a healing session. I invited the daughter to assist me by placing her hands lightly on her mother's back and asking for God's healing energy. When we finished, the daughter told her mom happily, "You got the green light!" In fact, the mother *had* seen green light as we worked on her, but her daughter insisted she hadn't seen it and didn't know why she'd even said such a thing.

Some clients were so profoundly touched by the healing energy that they sensed, or even saw, angels or spirits around them, and some experienced a deep connectedness to God. As I placed my hands on the shoulders of a schoolteacher named Charlee, hoping to ease her strained back and migraine headaches, she lay peacefully before me, then suddenly started to laugh. "My mother's here!" she exclaimed. "She said, 'Hello, Daughter.'" Charlee's father and a special cousin arrived next, and her cousin greeted her with a despised childhood nickname. To my surprise, Charlee suddenly snapped, "Don't call me Cheese!"

When my friend Kay asked if I could help her adult son, I discovered that healing energy also works over distances. She asked if I could work on him without his knowledge because she was pretty sure he wouldn't go for any hocus pocus, in spite of his worry about a lingering throat pain. His father had died from the effects of cancer not long before, and throat pain was an early symptom, so there was reason for concern. I cleared my mind, closed my eyes, visualized Kay's son before me, and reached out into thin air, placing my hands on his envisioned neck just as if he were there in the room with me. Within an hour of my work, he called his mom and announced that the pain in his throat had vanished. I learned two things that day: 1) just like prayer, you can send healing energy over any distance, and 2) just like prayer, the recipient doesn't even have to know it's being sent.

As fascinating as healing work was, and as much as it seemed to help with migraines and earaches and arthritis pain, I was frustrated because I had no way to know what ailments it would or wouldn't address. Every healing book I read was noticeably silent on this point. I was discouraged when people who refused to take any responsibility for their own self care came looking for a quick fix and dismayed when those truly in need of a miracle sought me out. Sometimes ailments disappeared immediately, sometimes healing came with time and several treatments, sometimes improvement was complete, sometimes it was partial, and sometimes the ailment didn't seem to respond at all. Since almost every client reported a sense of great peace and nearly everyone felt the warmth of the energy, I was confident that the healing work was always beneficial. I just couldn't predict in what ways and to what extent it would help, and that was hard to explain to people. I speculated that in the same way you wouldn't expect healing energy to re-grow a missing finger, no doubt some other kinds of damage are similarly irreparable.

When I asked Dr. Nu about the nature of healing energy, he told me it is *not* a miracle cure. It's a natural energy that works within natural laws to speed up the body's own healing processes. He warned me not to allow my ego to take responsibility for fixing any other person's physical or emotional needs, for this is the work of the individual. He was also clear that the process is not "faith healing," for its benefits are not dependent on either the healer's or the patient's faith in the healing process. I'd already discovered that fact when a skeptical woman with a headache sat down in my chair at the gardeners' market and announced that she didn't "believe in this stuff." She was only stopping, she said, because her husband insisted. It was fun to see the surprise on her face as her headache disappeared.

When a young father named Brad asked Dr. Nu whether stem cell therapy would be a beneficial treatment for his neurological disease, Charcot-Marie-Tooth Disorder (CMT), Dr. Nu replied that it would be beneficial for many ailments and that, yes, CMT would definitely be aided by stem cell therapy. He showed me an image of stem cells replacing and re-growing damaged nerve cells.

Dr. Nu observed that the only thing holding back research on stem cell therapy is our wrestling with the morality of using fetal stem cells, so I asked what *about* the morality of using fetal tissue? "Using stem cells would be a positive benefit resulting from some spirits' very short time in their human incarnations," he replied. Then he added, "Human researchers often think they alone are responsible for their discoveries and fail to perceive that they are supported and assisted by spirit. Human beings' perceptions are very limited."

When Dr. Nu speaks to my clients, he often addresses the spiritual issues surrounding their ailments. "Cancer does not preclude joy," he told a diminutive, gray-haired retiree named Ann as my hands rested lightly on her forehead and the top of her head. I spoke his words as he informed Ann that her third bout with ovarian cancer would not necessarily mean her departure from this Earth incarnation. "The result of this illness will be your heart's desire," he said. "The decision whether to go or stay will be made at the soul level, but not without input from your heart and mind." He encouraged Ann to turn her own healing powers on herself and reminded her, "Cancer is just an experience. It's part of your path."

Over and over, Dr. Nu encouraged my clients to recognize their own ability to direct God's healing energy to themselves and others. When he spoke to a retiree named Vickie, he confirmed her calling as a healer and gave her detailed information on how to sense and direct healing energy, stressing that the healer's loving intention for another is key to the healing process.

Dr. Nu told Lynn, a university professor who'd just been diagnosed with pancreatic cancer, to trust her doctors and follow their advice. He showed me an image of the cancer formed around a tube-like structure, and when the doctors operated, they found it located around the tube-like pancreatic duct. Dr. Nu revealed his gentle sense of humor when he assured Lynn, "You are on our prayer list." Unknown to me, Lynn's husband was working diligently to place her name on every prayer list he could find.

One November evening my friend Monica lay on my healing table as I rested my hands lightly on her elbow. I could feel the heat and pulsing sensation in my hands as the energy flowed to the pain that had plagued her for a year and a half. Suddenly, in my mind I heard a gentle voice say, "This is My beloved child, in whom I am well pleased." I knew instantly that the source of the message was not Dr. Nu or even Eia, but God, for the words were those He spoke at Jesus' baptism (Matthew 17:5), and they were unmistakable. (This quote was the one and only thing I'd retained from two years of pre-teen Saturday morning catechism classes.

Could it be that it stuck with me in preparation for just this moment of recognition?)

I delivered God's words to Monica, but when He told me I could tell her that after tonight the pain in her elbow would be gone, I hesitated, protesting that I didn't want to deliver this news in case it didn't turn out to be true. "You may tell her this," He repeated. Monica asked me why I was giggling.

"Because I'm arguing with God," I laughed, then told her what He'd said. Of course her pain disappeared.

I had one huge nagging question about healing and healers, and once I'd heard God's words for Monica, it occurred to me that maybe He would answer my question Himself, so one day I simply asked Him. "God," I began, "I've been wondering why You need healers. I mean, you're God. If You can heal someone, why don't You just *do* it? Just take the healing energy and deliver it to the place where it's needed."

A picture of a desert popped into my mind, and I heard that same loving voice say, "A tree can't grow in the desert."

I didn't get it. "Explain that to me," I said.

"A tree can't grow where the energy is not," the voice replied. "Where tree energy is not."

I still wasn't sure I understood, and asked, "So healing can't happen where healing energy is not?"

"Now you understand me," God replied.

"So healers are a way to bring the energy to where it's needed?" I asked.

"Exactly," God said. "As you suggested, I *am* just taking the healing energy and delivering it to the place where it's needed. *You* are My delivery mechanism."

"Wow!" I exclaimed.

"Exactly. I am 'just healing.' I'm doing it through your hands."

A few days later I asked God again about His use of healers. This time He told me, "You are the vessel that allows people to consciously help themselves." In other words, seeking the help of a healer is one way people can take responsibility for, and participate in, their own healing.

A couple of months later I visited my friends Susie and Greg in Alaska. As we discussed God's use of healers, Susie was reminded of the story about the man who's caught in a flood. As he sees the waters rising, the man says a prayer to God, announcing that he has complete trust that God will rescue him from the flood. As the waters rise, his neighbors offer to give him a ride out of the area in their big 4-wheel-drive vehicle. The man declines, confident that God will save him. A day later he's been forced to move to the second floor of his house. Looking out a second story window, he sees a rescue raft pass nearby. The people in the raft call out and offer him a ride to safety, but he declines, still certain that God will rescue him. As the water continues to rise, the man is stranded on his rooftop when a helicopter swoops down to gather him up. Once again he refuses, confident that his faith in God will ensure his rescue. Finally, the man is swept away by the still-rising water and drowns.

Arriving in heaven, the man insists on seeing God and demands to know why God did not show up to rescue him from the flood. God answers, "First I sent you a 4-wheel-drive vehicle, then I sent you a raft, and finally I even sent you a helicopter! What were you waiting for?"

It was exactly like God's explanation that healers are the delivery mechanism for His healing energy, but just in case I'd missed His point the first time, God repeated Himself. Two days later I was talking about my healing experiences with a woman on the plane from Fairbanks to Anchorage. She responded with the very same story Susie had told about the man in the flood!

Okay, God! I thought. *I got it. Healers are your emissaries, the guys in the 4-wheel-drive vehicle, the rescue raft, and the helicopter.*

16

T ime and again Dr. Nu encouraged my clients to cultivate and use their own healing abilities. The instructions he gave my client Vickie validated many of the healing techniques I had already discovered—no doubt with unrecognized input from Dr. Nu—and were so complete that, with her permission and only minor editing, I'm including them here for you. With loving intention for others, you, too, have the potential to be one of the guys in the 4-wheel-drive vehicle, the rescue raft, and the helicopter.

Vickie came to me for a reading with Eia because she had a feeling she was being called to do healing work. As I began to speak the spirit words I was receiving, however, it was Dr. Nu, not Eia, who weighed in.

"Vickie," he began, "you have come to us seeking information about your healing talents and abilities. You have always been a healer in a variety of ways, some more subtle than others. You are a peacemaker. You are a friend-maker. You are gentle to others in all circumstances, and this has been a hallmark of your personality since you were a child. You have a gift of healing touch. There is healing even in your glance. You have an ability to look with great kindness and great love on your fellow human beings, and the energy that is conveyed to them through you brings healing to their systems.

"You have asked about developing your healing technique. It is of course your decision which healing mode appeals to you. You are aware of Nyla Newman, who is a great Reiki master and teacher. Should you choose Reiki, we can recommend no one more highly than Nyla for your training. You have read the book *The Reconnection* by Eric Pearl, and this is another iteration of the same healing energy that does not require Reiki's special training. There are others whom you know, including Jan, who are laying on hands healers. Laying on hands is a technique that will come very naturally to you.

"So I will give you some guidance for laying on hands," Dr. Nu continued, "but first let me mention that there is healing in very simple forms of touch, everyday touch. There is healing in music. There is healing in tones. Healing energy is accessible through the use of crystals. Singing bowls. All of these modes are available to you, and any of them would be good channels for the healing energy that you naturally call to yourself and share with others around you.

"But now allow me to give you a little more instruction in what you may choose as a very straightforward initial mode to elaborate on, and this is 'the laying on of hands.' To employ this technique, it is important for you to calm your mind, close your eyes, and focus on your hands. Place them in your lap, palms up, and attend to them. Place your attention on your hands, and in prayer ask that God's healing energy be directed through your hands to those who are in need of it. With time if not immediately, as you become more finely attuned to the sensations in your hands, you will feel a slight buzz, a tingling, often heat, a sensation of warmth.

"If you need help at first to activate this sensation, a technique that we in spirit can recommend to you is to send your awareness heavenward and visualize a great cloud of healing energy that is then drawn down in beams of energy directly to the centers of your palms. Then you will begin to sense and visualize your hands pulsing and perhaps even glowing with this healing energy.

"It is a common exercise to hold your hands up, palms facing each other several inches apart, and move them closer and farther apart. In doing this you very soon will develop the ability to sense the energy connection between them, the energy flow between your palms. At some moments it will feel like they are attracting, and at other moments it will feel like they are repelling each other. This is a useful exercise to help yourself become sensitized to the existence of the energy. When you have had the opportunity to sense this energy about you and in your hands, when you are aware of it, it will be all the easier for you to direct it to the physical bodies of those who are in need of your touch.

"When someone comes to you or you are drawn together for a healing purpose," Dr. Nu continued, "take a few moments. Center and calm your mind. Do the simple visualization of light beams from the heavens to activate the energy flow through your hands, and then direct the energy to the place where it is most needed by ever-so-gently placing your hands on or above that location. It is not necessary to remove any clothing. It's not necessary for you to even touch the person to whom you are sending energy. It is also not critical that you find the exact and perfect spot, for this is very high, powerful energy. Trust me when I tell you it has an intelligence of its own and is very capable of distributing itself throughout the body to all the places where it is needed.

"If you are working with a person who does not have a particular location of pain or who may have emotional issues that you wish to address, a good location from which you may send energy to their entire system is, first and foremost, the top of their head, their crown, the seventh chakra if you are familiar with chakras and think in those terms. You may also place the other hand on the back of their neck or on their forehead or on their chest. These are several places from which, again, the energy can flow easily throughout their system.

"In actual fact, you could place your hands around their *toes* and have the same effect, but the psychological benefit of placing your hands in these very significant locations will be important to the process. It is very comforting for the person you are helping to receive your ministrations, and so your light and gentle touch is very calming and brings great peace in the process.

"Now I must tell you two other things. The first one is that the person you are working on does not even have to be physically present. You can send this energy across unlimited distances simply by calming your mind, inviting the energy in, thanking God for His gift of healing energy, and then visualizing the person before you as if he or she is lying on a massage table. Place your hands into the air, into the visualized location where you wish to send the energy, just as if they were before you in person, and the energy will have the same effect as if they were before you. In this scenario it is not even critical that the person know you are sending them healing energy. It will have the same good effect.

"The other important thing for me to tell you is that you must not consider this energy flow to be a miracle cure—although, indeed, there are some conditions that will be helped very quickly through this healing touch and the energy you convey. And as an aside, I might mention that you will become very good at healing your own headaches in a matter of seconds.

"It is important for you to know that the purpose of this healing energy is to activate the individual's own internal, personal healing energy. Your role is to provide a jump start to their own energy, and it is not your responsibility to cure every ailment or to solve every problem. This is the work of the individual, but you can have a great, deep, lasting beneficial effect.

"I would also mention to you that this is not faith healing, in that it is not dependent upon your faith or the faith of the person to whom you send the energy. In fact, the benefits of this energy are not even dependent on their belief in its efficacy. This energy exists, and it works, and it functions to the benefit of mankind, regardless of mankind's own intent.

"Bear in mind also that for some individuals, for their soul's purpose, healing is not the goal, so do not allow your ego to take on the responsibility to fix a person's physical or emotional needs. This is not the purpose of the healing energy. It is a natural energy that is a gift from God and will have great benefit whether or not a particular ill is quickly healed.

"Now I hope that I have not discouraged you, for indeed, this is a great gift for you to share with others. Your loving intention for another individual is one of the key links in the healing process. As the healer, your loving intention for the individual is a very important link in the healing process and in the delivery of healing energy.

"We who are in spirit honor and bless your work in every healing mode, from laying on hands to simple kindness. We recognize in you a great ability, and we encourage you to follow this impulse that you have felt tugging at your heart. Your interest in healing is applauded and strongly supported by us on the spirit side, and we thank you for your willingness to pursue it."

Then Dr. Nu asked, "Do you have questions, either for myself or for Eia?"

"I'm just wondering why it took so many years to figure this out," Vickie said. "Wouldn't it have helped a lot more people if I'd been able to discern this many years ago?"

"You sell yourself short," Dr. Nu replied. "I have already told you there is healing even in your glance, and this has been true throughout this Earth incarnation. You have been about other business, and throughout all of your family life, your work life, your church life, your recreation and leisure, throughout every aspect of your life, your healing touch has been active. Now you are asking for guidance in becoming more aware of it, and in becoming more aware of it, you increase your ability to direct it with conscious intent. But make no mistake. It has been very much with you and has benefitted countless friends, family, and acquaintances throughout your lifetime to this point. Now especially, because you are past much of the busywork of the earlier phases of your life, you are able to cultivate your abilities to manipulate and direct healing energy. This is a good time for you to begin to intensify your interests and activity in the healing realm."

"Can you give me a clear picture of what the clouds and the rays should look like?" Vickie asked. "I'm struggling with conjuring a strong, clear image."

Dr. Nu explained. "As you use visualization to become sensitized to the presence of this energy, sit quietly and still your mind. Place your hands in your lap with the palms up, and with your eyes closed, picture your palms and imagine a glowing sphere of golden light in each one of them. See it moving gently in the palm of your hand. That alone may be enough to bring to your attention the sensation of energy. If it is not, with your palms still up in your lap, cast your mind upward and simply picture a cloud of golden or white or blue light. Seeing a sort of gently-glowing cloud, ask for this healing energy to flow from the heavens to your hands. Allow a picture to form of energy simply drawing gently and glowingly down as if in a beam of light into the palms of your hands."

"So is it better if I'm outside?" Vickie asked.

"It's not necessary," Dr. Nu replied. "In fact, the exact form of the visualization is not critical. I simply suggest this image as a way to picture for yourself that there is a healing energy around you and above you in the universe. In reality, of course, it pervades everything, but the human mind often thinks in terms of 'heaven,' and hence I suggest the idea of a cloud above you. It might be pink. Then, with your mind always thankful and appreciative for God's gift of healing, ask for God's healing energy to be directed to your hands and through your hands to the place where it is needed.

"Picture the energy flowing to you as light beaming into the palms of your hands. And again, you might move your hands in little circular motions. That may help you begin to perceive that little hum of energy. You might also sense it as warmth or as a tingling, but especially early in your work with this energy, it will probably feel like a tiny little buzz throughout your palms and fingers. Be aware that it may sometimes intensify greatly, but that's not necessary. Indeed, it is not even necessary that you feel it, that you have the sensation of energy in order for you to direct this healing energy to yourself or others. Knowing that it is there and is available to you, gratefully asking for it to be directed through your hands, is enough. As you do this more often, the sensation will come. Feeling the energy is partly a process of your brain becoming sensitized to the sensation. At first it may be more subtle than what you are expecting."

"I have found it impossible to see anybody else's auras," Vickie said, "and I'm wondering if there's some kind of block or resistance in my mind. If there is and I could overcome it, would it be useful in this healing? Or is there even a connection?"

"The ability to see auras is not by any means a prerequisite to making a beneficial use of the universe's healing energy," Dr. Nu told her. "Indeed, in many ways, unless you become highly proficient at interpreting the auras of others, it is often of little more use than a parlor trick. Having said that, if you are interested in pursuing the ability to see auras, my best suggestion is that you stand your 'victim' against a neutral-colored wall, for that is one of the keys that is most helpful when beginning to learn this ability. A light colored, neutral background will go a long way toward helping you develop the ability to sense auras," Dr. Nu concluded, "but this ability is not a requirement for healing work."

. . . .

To Dr. Nu's words I can only add that I have seen plenty of evidence to support his statement that God's healing energy is an intelligent energy, a powerful healing agent that distributes itself throughout the patient's body to address needs of all kinds. As healers we sometimes place our faith in rituals or gestures or incantations, creating a sense of dependence on words or actions that, in reality, are utterly superfluous to the healing process. It is simply our love that opens the door to God's healing energy, and no misstep or omission on our part could possibly undermine the effectiveness of God's healing power.

17

Almost as soon as she convinced me to lay hands on Dad's war wounds, Mom started urging me to work on animals. First she'd show me the image of an elephant (meaning "don't forget"), then my hands would begin to hum with energy ("heal"), then came pictures of every kind of animal from cats and dogs to buffaloes and giraffes: "Don't forget to heal animals."

To be honest, I was more interested in *talking* to animals than healing them, but I wasn't having any success at it. Day after day I sat on the couch with Jock, sent out my thoughts to him, and waited for an image in reply, but there was no response. I'd received the white horse's "lonely" message loud and clear, and our golden retriever, Buddy, had sent me images of swimming in the ocean and doggie sex, so I couldn't figure out why I wasn't connecting with Jock. When a journalist friend named Jennifer invited me over to see whether my healing energy could reduce her dog's aggression toward other canines, it turned into a healing session *and* a doggie conversation.

A pretty mixed breed dog with long, soft brown and black fur, Sis was a regular troublemaker, starting fights with other dogs almost daily. As I sat with her, moving my hands over her body, focusing my energy and asking for God's healing touch, I wondered whether the healing energy would help with aggression. Sis was clearly a sweet and loving dog with humans, and it was lovely just to sit with her and sink my fingers into her soft fur.

As we sat quietly together, a little movie suddenly popped into my mind. I saw a dog's-eye view of chasing a squirrel across their backyard. It had to be from Sis. She'd sent me a message! I seized the opportunity and mentally told Sis that Jennifer loves her very much. In my mind I heard her happy answer, "I know." I told her she's beautiful, and she replied, "I know. My mom tells me that." I had to laugh. It was the first time I'd experienced animals' lack of false modesty, and I was charmed.

Sis proceeded to give me a visual tour of her world, showing me that she often tips over her water bowl, showing how she hops into the front seat of the car before jumping into the back, and hinting that she'd like to sleep on her mom and dad's bed.

When I assured Sis that Jennifer loves her and she doesn't have to fight with other dogs, Sis replied, "They should stay away from my mom." I promised that Jennifer will always love her best and told Sis that if she didn't fight with other dogs, she'd be able to play with them. "I don't care," Sis replied. "I want them to go away." Then she added, "And no other dogs should come to our house." Clearly Sis wasn't getting the idea, so I sent her lots of images of running and playing happily with other dogs, then returning to Jennifer for hugs and kisses.

The next time I saw Jennifer, she told me Sis's behavior with other dogs had improved so dramatically that two different people had asked her, "Is that the same dog you used to have?"

That was great, but the bigger discovery for me was how much of Sis's communication was verbal! I never expected a dog's thoughts to come through to me in words, so I'd been sending Jock images and waiting for images in return. Now I sat down on the couch beside Jock and sent him a question in plain English. "What do you do all day while I'm at work?" I asked.

Instantly a thought popped into my mind, and it, too, was verbal: "I sleep on all the beds!" I was so surprised that I laughed out loud and headed straight for the guest room. Jock refuses to jump onto the bed even when I beg him to, but sure enough, there, next to the pillow on each of the guest beds, was a Jock-sized indentation.

A few days later my friend Peggy challenged me to see if I could talk with her big golden retriever, Kipper. Making the connection was easy and, once again, largely verbal. I asked Kipper if there was anything he'd like to tell Peggy, and he said, "When you open the refrigerator, I can help you. I can show you what I like to eat." He showed me a picture of butter and added, "Butter would be good."

I laughed and told Peggy what he'd said. "He's really fixated on the refrigerator," I added. "Does he actually pay attention when you open it?" None of our dogs did.

"Oh, absolutely," she said. "When he hears the refrigerator door open, he can be outside, and he'll come whoopin' in here."

Kipper chimed in, "There's more stuff I could eat," and sent me an image of a fish filet.

"He's talking about fish," I told Peggy. "Do you have fish in the fridge?"

"We're having fish filets for dinner," she said. "They're defrosting on the counter."

When I asked Kipper if there was anything he needed Peggy to do for him, and he showed me a picture of a blanket and sent the idea that he'd like her to wash and dry his blankets to make them fluffier. "Do you ever do that?" I asked.

"I do it every week," Peggy said, "but I didn't do it today. Now I'm sad that I didn't. I usually do, but I thought, 'This is okay. He can sleep on it another week.' That's so funny! Kipper, I'll wash it tomorrow."

The conversation was delightful. Showing me a picture of the backyard, Kipper said, "That's my house, too. This whole house is my house, and I'm in charge. I make sure that everything is safe. I make sure the cat can go out when she wants to. I tell my mom when the cat needs to go out, and she listens to me." Then he confided, "The cat is kind of dumb. The cat doesn't know I'm doing that for her, but I do it anyway because I'm in charge, and that's my job." Then he told Peggy, "You're getting up too early. You need to stay in bed because when you get up, I have to get up."

"To get the paper," Peggy said. "We can't do anything until you get the paper."

"That's my present to you in the morning," Kipper responded, "but I don't like to do that. That's not a dog job."

"That *is* a dog job," Peggy protested. "It's the only real job you have."

"No, I'm in charge of the whole house," Kipper repeated, "and I'm good at it."

The whole conversation was fun and crazy and full of information I couldn't have known in advance. I was thrilled!

It turns out that animals will tell you all kinds of things if you just ask them. They'll tell you what they like and don't like, what they need, what they fear and why, and what their favorite food is. A German shepherd named Patch loves to sit in the car in the driveway but is terrified when the car moves through traffic. When I asked why, he sent me pictures of cars zooming in from every direction. It was enough to scare me, too. So why does he sit in the car for hours in the driveway? According to Patch, he's waiting for his owner, Nancy. Driving is the only time he gets her to himself.

When I asked a big long-haired male cat to tell me a secret, I saw a picture of him disappearing under the dust ruffle of a double bed. This was followed by an image of him on his back under the bed, scratching the bottom of the box springs. His owner laughed and assured me it wasn't a secret, that he'd torn out the entire bottom of their last box springs.

My niece Glori, an art teacher, once asked me to talk to her young cat Dakini about her habit of relieving herself on the dining room throw rugs instead of using the litter box. As I drove over to Glori's house, I heard a voice in my mind. "I'm Butch!" it said. "I'm smaller, but I'm tough." I saw a picture of a tortoiseshell cat lying on top of some socks on a bedroom floor. When Glori confirmed that Dakini has tortoiseshell coloring, is the smaller of her two cats, and loves to lie on top of her roommate's dirty socks, I told her, "In that case, Dakini wants you to know that her name is really Butch!"

Most animals seem to really appreciate the opportunity to communicate with their humans, and the owners often comment on how calm their dog or cat seems while I talk with them. I've been nuzzled by usually-skittery horses, and I've been sat on by cats who never came near a stranger in their lives. My brother Dave and his wife Louie have a black cat named Batty who is as shy of strangers as they come. Over the years I'd caught occasional glimpses of Batty as she peeked at me, then fled to safety under some upstairs bed. When Louie asked me to come and talk with Batty, I urged her not to stress Batty out by bringing her downstairs and into the living room where I was sitting. Lo and behold, Batty strolled right in and flopped over onto her side for a tummy rub from her mom. Before I arrived, Louie had told Batty that if she had anything to say, she should come downstairs and say it to me while I was there. We had a very helpful chat, during which I encouraged Batty not to freak out at the construction noises as Dave and Louie expanded their house. The next thing I knew, Batty jumped up into my arms, buried her head under my elbow, and purred!

When my Aunt Sandy asked if I could find out how her horse injured her back, I discovered that, like healing energy, animal communication also works long distance. I sat on my own backyard deck in Utah and sent out my thoughts to her 19-year-old bay mare, Patti Jo Springtime, 1,500 miles away in Indiana. Patti Jo's response was almost immediate, and she showed me exactly what had happened. She was stung on her left side by an insect and jumped sideways. When she jumped, she fell forward onto her knees and had trouble getting back up again. Sandy told me they have hornets in their horse corral and, sure enough, she'd recently found a large welt on Patti Jo's left side.

Anxious for more opportunities to practice, I invited myself over to try talking with the two horses owned by Natalie, the 14-year-old whose fainting spells I'd worked on. Natalie wanted to know whether Dusty, the older horse, likes their dressage riding lessons. "The teacher is kind of tough," Dusty told me. "She claps at me."

I looked at Natalie. "The teacher *claps* at him?" I asked. It's true. When Dusty hesitates at a jump, the teacher walks up behind him and gives a loud clap to get him moving.

Natalie, the horses, and I talked and talked—about their horse trailer, the farrier, mountain trail rides, fly spray, why Thumper doesn't like men, and whether Thumper would like a goat for company when Natalie takes Dusty to 4-H horse camp for three days. "No goats," he said. "Goats are dumb."

The last image I received was a cracked hoof, a cracked left front hoof. Natalie called me later to say she'd checked all eight of their hooves without finding any problems. After scouting around, however, she'd discovered that the neighbors' horse across the fence had a left front hoof cracked so badly it was bleeding. Did the neighbor horse send me the message himself? I don't know. I like to think that Dusty sent word on his behalf.

18

E ven as my healing clientele grew, I began to understand why my move to Indiana and full time healing work hadn't materialized. Eia, my spirit guide, told me that my primary spiritual work would not be healing, but channeling the words of spirits for individuals seeking guidance in their lives. The more spirit messages I delivered, the more I saw her point. It was fascinating and fun, and my clients found Eia's counseling loving and wise.

Almost as soon as I met Eia, my friend Evelyn and I started getting together so I could practice channeling. In one of our first sessions, Evelyn inquired about a nephew who'd been in a car accident. I saw a picture of a wheelchair and got the feeling that there was some doubt whether the young man would ever walk again. That stopped me in my tracks as I thought, *Don't say that. If that's wrong, it will be* so *wrong.* My ego didn't want me to make a mistake. Naturally, when I finally asked Evelyn whether there was a question of her nephew walking again, she said, "Oh, very much so." Like the identifiers from loved ones who've passed on, Eia's messages usually have identifiers of their own—things I couldn't have known or guessed.

Once when Evelyn asked whether Eia had any closing message for her, all I got was a picture of a big, beautiful bunch of broccoli. No words, no explanation, just broccoli. When I said, "All I'm getting is a big bunch of broccoli," Evelyn laughed and told me she's a broccoli fanatic. She eats it almost every day for lunch. I guess it was Eia's way of putting a stamp of authenticity on our session, an identifier to assure us both that I hadn't made up the message.

Clients brought Eia their questions about love and life, family and career, past lives and spirit guides, and she answered them all with a kindness so profound even I was touched. She taught that we are not alone on life's path, there are no lessons that must be learned, and there is no force for evil in the world beyond what man inflicts upon himself. "The purpose of life," she said time and again, "is simply to experience the joy of living, to experience your true nature as a being of love and light, and as God's child." She encourages us to hold only kind thoughts for one another, saying, "Human beings have no idea how powerful they are in their ability to effect positive change in the world through the energy they send out."

As a "conscious channel," I'm wide awake and listening in as I convey Eia's messages to my clients. Being a conscious channel, however, can be a problem. As I listen for Eia's words, my mind keeps working in the background, making observations that are sometimes helpful but more often distracting. It's an ongoing struggle to shush the running commentary. More than once Eia has told me, "Your busy mind holds you back," and when I ask her for tips on how to improve my channeling, she says, "Don't listen." Don't listen to the words coming out of my mouth? Yeah, right. On good days I get in a groove and simply speak Eia's words without first hearing and then repeating them. I know that's the way it's supposed to be done, but it takes a lot of practice—and a *lot* of trust.

I've discovered only two kinds of questions Eia really doesn't answer. She rarely responds to medical queries, and she usually declines to predict the future. When a client asks, "Will I ever get married again?" or "Will I move to Oregon?" she typically replies, "Well you know, your choices are your own, and the future is not set in stone." I have to warn clients in advance that Eia is not a fortune teller.

Actually, there's one more kind of information Eia doesn't give: lottery numbers. The only time anyone asked her for the lucky numbers, Eia replied, "I'm sorry, but you have to pick those yourself. Good luck!"

Once an animal-loving high school student asked Eia for some career guidance. She was considering vet school but leaning toward wildlife management. Eia wisely pointed out the likelihood that a career in wildlife management would involve managing fish and game populations for the benefit of hunters and fishermen!

When another client asked Eia how he'll know when he attains enlightenment, I felt her smile kindly before observing that human beings often think reaching enlightenment "is like your fairy godmother bonking you on the head with her magic wand." Rather, she explained, it's about growing your ability to live consciously, learning to maintain an awareness of your own true identity as a being of love and light and energy. "When you can hold this awareness even as you move through your human existence," Eia told him, "then you will have attained enlightenment."

As each reading begins, Eia typically opens with some comments of her own, then asks the client what they'd like to talk about. People are amazed when she starts a reading by answering questions they haven't even asked yet or comments on topics they hadn't intended to bring up.

When my fun and outgoing friends Jim and Kelly came over for a reading, Eia opened the conversation by talking to Jim about his work as an engineer with an aerospace corporation. Eia noted that he was being groomed to move up in management, then suggested that he might prefer to move into a training position instead. She observed that a training job would satisfy his desire to teach without having to continue teaching college classes on the side. Then she said, "Your wife is nodding." I opened my eyes to see Kelly nodding her head. Kelly laughed and said she'd just told Jim the very same thing, and Jim said it was as if I'd been reading his e-mail for the last two days. In fact, he'd just been approached about moving into the company's training division, while his current boss urged him to stay put.

Like the folks who seek healing without taking any responsibility for their own well-being, some people come to Eia seeking approval for their bad behavior—usually adulterous relationships. Eia gently reminds them that their decisions impact many lives. More than one client has spent their entire reading trying to convince Eia they're in the right. At moments like those I'm glad the message is coming from Eia and not from me. When I yearn to snap, "Shut up and listen," Eia says simply, "Hear me now."

My friend Nyla, a bubbly and energetic nurse and a healer herself, was the first person to ask Eia about a past incarnation. A previous psychic told her she'd lived in wartime France, and Eia agreed on that. She described how Nyla had taken her cat and traveled on foot and by canal to Belgium. There she settled in the city of Liege and worked for a family as a nanny or tutor. As Eia narrated the story, she showed me images of a young woman walking with a cat in her arms and chatting with a boy as he petted the cat. While the story and images were fascinating, I had one big problem with the details. I seemed to recall that Liege is located in France, rather than Belgium.

Eia continued, saying that late in this previous lifetime, Nyla worked as a cleaning woman in a Liege cathedral and ultimately was buried in the churchyard. Nyla immediately asked, "What's the name?" meaning the name on the headstone. I misunderstood the question and sent Eia the thought, *What's the name of the cathedral?,* to which she replied, "St. Bartholomew's."

The next day I checked the internet to verify the location of Liege. Naturally, it *is* located in Belgium. And one of the city's historical highlights? St. Bartholomew's Church, of course, built in the 11th and 12th centuries.

Unfortunately, some topics Eia raises are not verifiable by any means. I was dismayed when Eia told a tall, serious young man named Andy that his interest in Native American culture stems from two past lives, the first as an Iroquois Indian, the second a hundred years later as a Cherokee. Though she gave details about his role in each tribe and his relationships to his

Indian family members, nothing Eia said was verifiable, and it seemed terminally corny to tell someone he'd been a wise and respected Iroquois leader and then a child on the Cherokees' Trail of Tears, wearing holes in the moccasins his grandmother had made for him. In a funny way, though, it confirmed for me that I wasn't making it up because it seemed so ridiculously unbelievable, I never would have said it.

For Andy, the reading was validated when Eia told him he would soon have a new pair of moccasins, a pair that might even be made by a man. They would be decorated with green floral beadwork. In fact, Andy was already making himself a new pair of moccasins, and he'd just begun the beadwork—an emerald green floral design.

Even as she offers her loving perspective and support, Eia encourages people to contact their own spirit guides directly. She brought two college coeds, Emily and Natali, news of a deceased brother and a beloved grandmother, then told them, "This is our gift to you from those of us who are on the Other Side: we assure you that you are loved, you are cherished, you are safe and secure, and we invite you to communicate with us. We invite your communication, and we pledge that we will always answer you. Our answer may come to you as a thought or a feeling, in the words of the next song you hear, in a passage of a book you're reading, or in a chance conversation. Often our communication will sound to you like your own imagination or your own ideas, but you will know it is from us when it takes you by surprise and brings you ideas that you did not expect or have never thought before. Then you will know that you are not imagining our communication from the Other Side.

"You have such goodness in you," Eia continued. "You human beings have no idea how good you are. Know that you are loved and that you are full of light and love and peace. Remember that we in spirit will talk to you any time you wish."

Eia invites us to communicate with our spirit guides, but she also encourages us to communicate with each other in ways we seldom think about in these high tech times. When clients ask how they can help a sick or struggling friend or loved one, Eia often urges them to send written notes and even postcards. She reminds us that in these days of electronic communication, a tangible message of love and support in our own handwriting—something that can be read and re-read, touched, and held—can mean everything to the person who receives it.

We're used to human communication, but you never know what form a message from the Other Side may take. An older man once approached me, disappointed that he hadn't heard from his recently deceased wife. Friends and family were all telling him to watch and listen for her to get in touch. One day as he spoke with his daughter on the phone, his young granddaughter in the background asked, "Is that Grandpa? Tell him Grandma says hi." Instead of bringing comfort, it made him feel worse that even his little granddaughter had heard from Grandma while he still hadn't received a message himself. I encouraged him to watch for subtle signs that indicate she is still with him—the bloom of a favorite flower, a flickering light, notes from an un-wound music box. Only later did I slap my forehead as I realized that *of course* the message via his granddaughter *was* the message he was waiting for!

When Judy, an environmental policy specialist, talked with Eia, she'd been invited to apply for an important post in Washington, D.C. With a husband and two small children to consider, she felt unable to leap at the opportunity to have a truly significant impact on environmental policy and issues.

Eia addressed her concern in an amazing reading, announcing that Judy is a very high spirit who has come to Earth at this time to impact man's relationship with the environment and to assist human beings as they grow in their understanding of their responsibility to and for the Earth. Eia told Judy that she needn't regret not pursuing the big appointment because she is working "at the spirit level" and having tremendous influence no matter where she is or what job she is doing. Judy's teaching, Eia said, is having great impact on the human-environment connection by communicating to many people who then communicate to others.

But even more than that, at the soul level Judy is sending out waves of teaching, loving, healing energy that literally encircle the globe, positively affecting the human race's relationship to the environment.

As I channeled Eia's words for more and more people, I came to know her themes: gentleness and loving-kindness for each other, for ourselves, and for our world. If we could only live up to her belief in our goodness, we would indeed change the world.

19

As satisfying as it is to do healing work and to channel Eia and Dr. Nu, I enjoy mediumship even more because every identifier sent by the spirits reconfirms—not just for the client, but for me—that the contact is real. Even after hundreds of readings, I still crave the reassurance that it's not my imagination. When a spirit says "beret" and my client's jaw drops because her brother always wore one, I'm both delighted and relieved. When a spirit sends me the thought "empty gas tank" and my client tells me they ran out of gas on their first date, I'm thrilled.

Many spirit messages are so faint and fleeting that it's difficult to trust the vague impressions received. Thankfully, the more readings I did, the more I perceived words and ideas in addition to the pictures. It takes a lot of faith in the spirits and in the process—and a lot of practice—to describe what you're seeing and hearing without judging or interpreting it.

When my friend Jim's aunt sent me the idea "goldfish," I told him she must have kept goldfish in a bowl or aquarium, but she hadn't. Only later did he remember the overgrown goldfish in the hot springs they often visited. My inserting a fish *bowl* into the message almost kept Jim's aunt from sharing a great memory—and a great identifier—with him. In another reading, I got a clear impression of a man with a major garage fixation and told my client that her father must have had a real attachment to his garage. A skeptic, she rejected the idea and only later told me that her *grandfather* practically lived in the garage. It was my mistake for reading "father" into the message.

Some mediumistic readings begin with a few "misses," images or ideas that the client doesn't recognize. It's like tuning in a radio station, honing in on the signal. I'm sure there are many reasons for the misses, first of which is my not accurately understanding or translating what the spirit is sending. For example, I once insisted to a client that the spirit was sending the image of a court jester, complete with bells on his pointy hat. It didn't ring any bells for her. When he sent me an image of a donkey, she didn't recognize that, either. When he sent the donkey image a second time, it came with the words, "I was a jackass!" Later it dawned on me that instead of "jester," he was probably trying to get me to say "fool."

I'd been reading *What Horses Say* about animal communicator Julie Dicker when a retiree named JoAnn arrived hoping to hear from her dear friend Ron. Ron got in touch, all right, but JoAnn didn't recognize any of the identifiers he sent—a dark-colored older car, a jar of pickles, the phrase "bed of roses," a jar of homemade jam. My stress level rose as she kept saying, no ... no ... no, so when I saw a running horse, I told myself not to even say it. I thought I must be imagining the horse because of the book I was reading when she arrived. Then Ron sent me a picture of a rocking horse. "A rocking horse?" I suggested doubtfully.

"That *might* make a connection," JoAnn allowed.

Afterwards JoAnn told me Ron's favorite thing in the world was to go to the horse races. Poor Ron, he must have figured a rocking horse was the only way he could get me to let the word "horse" come out of my mouth! As for the misses, JoAnn and Ron met later in life, so it's possible she simply didn't know what the images meant to him. Identifiers can be especially difficult when the client hopes to hear from someone they didn't know well.

Sometimes I have to stick with a message I'm sure of, even when the client doesn't recognize it. I can't tell you how many times someone has called or e-mailed after a reading to say they just remembered what an image or a message was referring to.

One of my favorite after-the-fact validations dawned on a woman named Sheila a couple of days after her reading. Her father had come through loud and clear from the Other Side, full of love and cheery news. "Your mom's busy running around over here," he said. "She's on every committee and singing in the choir."

When I asked for an identifier, he sent me a picture of a green pickup truck. Sheila laughed and said, "Yes, Dad, I still have your green truck!"

When I got the feeling that a raccoon was somehow associated with the truck, nothing clicked for Sheila. "Did a raccoon get into the truck?" I suggested. "Did he run over a raccoon? Did he have a pet raccoon that rode in the truck with him?" Sheila couldn't think of a single raccoon connection. Two days later it came to her, and she called to tell me that her daughter drove the green truck for two years, and the whole time, she had "a ratty old raccoon tail" hanging from the rearview mirror.

In a reading for my friend Mary Ann, one relative after another made themselves known, but she couldn't figure out why I kept getting images of gray Confederate Civil War uniforms. "All *my* relatives were Yankees," she insisted. The next day she called to say she'd talked with her mom and found out there were, in fact, plenty of Confederates hiding in the branches of the family tree.

The more readings I did, the more I realized that not everything I read in books by other mediums was necessarily true for me. For example, the common wisdom says that you can't guarantee that any given spirit will come through in a particular reading. You just have to invite them to show up and hope for the best. Frustrated by the misses at the beginning of readings, I started asking clients to give me just the first name of a spirit they hoped to hear from. When I ask for the spirit by name, they almost invariably come through. On the other hand, we doubtless miss some connections when Grandma Addie sends "key lime pie" and we fail to recognize her because we're asking for Uncle Bill.

When my friend Monica asked me to try to contact someone named Pat, a teddy bear, a silver convertible, and the words "He really is that nice" came through loud and clear. Then Pat added, "I sent him to you." It turned out that Monica was dating Pat's widower, Clark. His house was still filled with Pat's teddy bears, and he once gave Pat a gift of a convertible. Monica had been a bit nervous about their new relationship because Clark simply seemed too good to be true, but now she could relax knowing both that Pat approved of their relationship and that Clark really is that nice. To top it off, Monica called the next day to say she'd checked with Clark, and the convertible he gave Pat was, indeed, silver.

Sometimes spirits go beyond greetings and reassurances and touch on topics with huge significance, topics like euthanasia. When a young woman named Darcy hoped to hear from her recently-deceased Aunt Edith, I sent out a mental call: "Aunt Edith for Darcy." The first thing I heard was "Evanston," and sure enough, Aunt Edith was born and lived most of her life in Evanston, Wyoming. When the strange combination of "car" and "bunny" came through, Darcy recalled the time her young son's missing pet rabbit was found under a seat in the car.

When I heard the word "encephalitis," I wondered if Aunt Edith was trying to tell me how she died, but I doubted that anyone in Wyoming dies of encephalitis these days, so instead of just delivering the message, I asked whether someone had died of an unusual disease. Darcy told me Edith died of emphysema, and I said, "Oh, that must be what she was trying to tell me. I thought I heard 'encephalitis.'" It turned out Darcy's sister died of encephalitis.

Next Aunt Edith showed me a hospital room, and I heard the words, "They turned off my oxygen." Darcy confirmed that it was true.

"So they withdrew her life support?" I asked.

"They turned off her oxygen," Darcy told me. "That's how they did it."

Aunt Edith assured Darcy that she's fine and didn't suffer. She urged Darcy to stop feeling guilty, to let go of the guilt. She said, "The decision [to turn off my oxygen] was not yours to make, and it was the right decision at the time. I was just waiting to be released from my body."

Sometimes spirits show up before their humans arrive for their readings. Mary Ann of the Confederate ancestors gathered a few friends for a group reading, and before they arrived, I began to get images of parrots. One woman in the group, Mary, did indeed have a deceased friend who used to own a parrot. When I gave the parrot-owning spirit the go-ahead, she sent me the idea that she'd had a favorite car. Mary wasn't sure, but when I heard "Jeep," she laughed and said, "Oh, yeah! She loved Jeeps!" In fact, she'd owned three Jeeps at once and had even given one to Mary. That was the entire message, "parrot" and "Jeep," but it was enough to get her meaning across: "I'm not dead!"

Next a spirit by the name of Ned came through. Ned was Mary Ann's adoptive father, but instead of sending a message for his daughter, he had news for another member of the group, a young mother named Martha. There's a great aunt of hers on the Other Side, Ned said. The aunt's initial is S. When Martha didn't know who that would be, the spirit aunt indicated an attachment to a male with the initial H, and Martha said that would probably be her great-great-grandfather Hillard. The next thing I saw was a map of Montana indicating the area around Butte, and sure enough, he was a Finn who immigrated to Montana and worked in the mines around Butte. When Hillard mentioned the name Robert with a connection to potatoes, Martha recalled that just before Hillard died, he and her father, Robert, had planted a big potato patch together.

Oddly, each time Martha said "Hillard," I heard what sounded like an echo from the Other Side. Every time she said "Hillard," someone else said "Hillyard," with a Y sound in it. When I finally mentioned it, Martha said, yes, his name actually was Hillyard. The family just pronounces it Hillard! There's nothing like being corrected from the Other Side. Later, when

Martha consulted her living relatives, she discovered that Hillyard's daughter's name was Sylvia—making her a great aunt with the initial S.

As we were winding up the session, I asked whether there were any other spirits waiting to communicate with the group. I immediately heard the name "Theodore," but nobody claimed him. No one had a Theodore, a Teddy, or a Ted. Then I heard a female name that began with E-L. Somebody had an Ellen, and someone else had a Helen, but this was a longer name. Still no takers. When I heard it again, I realized an *Eleanor* was trying to get through to me. As I spoke the name "Eleanor," I heard "Ted" again from my left, and the combination suddenly clicked. It was my own great aunt and uncle, Eleanor and Ted. The message was for me!

The same group got together two weeks later, and just like before, I began receiving information even before they arrived. This time I clearly heard the name Elmer. As we began the reading, Elmer told me he had a name connection to one of Martha's young sons. Sure enough, Elmer was a favorite uncle of Martha's husband, and one of their sons is named for him.

Toward the end of the session, a quiet woman named Laura asked me to try and contact a spirit named Eric. I closed my eyes and asked Eric to tell me who he was. When he indicated that he was a relative, I asked him to identify his place on a visualized family tree. Eric showed himself directly below Laura with a line connecting himself to her. "Your son?" I asked, and was surprised when she said no. The connection seemed so clear, I had to stifle the urge to ask, "Are you sure?"

It turned out Eric was her grandson. He told me he'd suffered from a head or brain ailment but had died of Sudden Infant Death Syndrome, SIDS. "That's absolutely correct," Laura told us.

One afternoon as I sent healing energy to my friend Charlie's arthritis pain, his mother came through with some fun identifiers and kidded him about a pair of oversized galoshes. Charlie laughed and recalled that after throwing rocks and breaking a garage window with some buddies, he was the only boy who got caught because he couldn't run fast enough in those darned galoshes. His mom reminded him about raccoon hunting and raising rabbits, loving hot dogs, and a green late 1940's Buick. Then she proudly told me, "Charlie chased a bear!" and he confirmed that, yes, he had, back in his days as a Michigan state trooper. The identifier that really got Charlie's attention was the phrase "raspberry tart." His mom always made his favorite tarts with her leftover pie dough. All of the identifiers, however, were just a prelude to her most important message: "Your Army son will be safe. I'm looking after him."

When I sat next to an accountant named Melavadene on a flight from Salt Lake City to Detroit, she noticed I was reading one of John Edward's books, and we struck up a conversation. In moments her deceased husband, Bill, was bragging to me, "I got you two together!"

Bill wanted me to tell Melavadene it's time to move on. "I appreciate your loyalty," he said, "but it's time to get the hospital stuff out of the house." Bill was paralyzed for more than eleven years, and now, a year and a half after his passing, Melavadene admitted she'd just been moving all the medical equipment into one room.

Bill told me that Melavadene had been thinking about a sporty car and let her know that he approved. In fact, she'd just sold the handicapped van and bought herself a brand new set of wheels.

It's funny, but I often get spirit messages while I'm traveling. I suppose my mind is less occupied with busywork when I'm away from my usual routine. Enjoying some ravioli between planes in Minneapolis, I once clearly heard the name "Joe." I looked around at the couple hundred fellow travelers and had no idea who the spirit Joe might belong to. I heard it again and considered the young man sitting kitty-corner from me across the table. How crazy would I sound if I said, "Excuse me, but do you know any dead guys by the name of Joe?" I decided not to bother. The message could be for anybody. Then I heard, "Jack" and "Joe-Jack, Joe-Jack, Joe-Jack." Okay, I had to mention it, but

I waited until I was finished with my meal. As I picked up my tray to go, I said to the young man, "Excuse me. I'm a college professor [not strictly true, but I figured it sounded better than college librarian], but I'm also a psychic. I'm hearing the names Joe and Jack. You don't happen to know any deceased people by those names, do you?"

He thought a moment, then shook his head and said, "Nope."

Retreating with my tray, I said, "Sorry, never mind. It could be for anyone around here." Talk about embarrassing. Back in the air and halfway to Salt Lake City, I slapped my forehead. My ex-husband's grandparents were Jo—for Josephine—and Jack!

I did most of my readings at home, where Jock barked enthusiastically when a client rang the doorbell, then settled down peacefully as the reading began. Settled down peacefully, that is, until Denny arrived. Tall and slender, in his late twenties, Denny showed up for a reading one snowy evening with a long list of departed friends he hoped to hear from. One after another they came through with identifiers and messages and characteristic turns of phrase that Denny easily recognized. It would have been a great reading except for Jock's insistent whining. He was upset about something and tried his best to convince me to leave Denny and go upstairs. Jock was so distressed that he even tried to climb over the arm of the chair and into my lap, something he never, ever does. It was totally out of character, and I had no idea why he was so upset.

The next morning when all was calm, I sat on the couch next to Jock and asked what was going on during Denny's reading. "Why were you so nervous last night?" I asked. "Were there spirits here?"

"They were all around him," Jock answered telepathically. Curious, since I'd never seen a spirit myself, I asked what they looked like, and Jock answered, "They look like people."

"You know, they won't hurt you," I tried to reassure him.

"I don't like them," he replied. "They're not real people."

Now I was really curious and asked, "Has this happened before, spirits coming here with people?"

"Often," Jock said.

"Do the spirits like you?" I asked.

"Some do," he told me, "but I don't like them."

"You know, they won't hurt you," I repeated.

"I don't care," Jock said. "I want them to go away."

"Do they ever talk to you?" I asked, and was surprised when he told me, "I can't hear them."

"Just remember that they won't hurt you," I repeated. "Those were Denny's friends who only wanted to talk to him."

To this Jock sensibly replied, "Then they should stay at his house!"

20

I n spite of my modest success with mediumship, healing, channeling, and animal communication, I was hardly a woo-woo prodigy. Racing through one woo-woo book after another, I found plenty of other psychic avenues to explore, but trying something and being good at it are different things entirely.

Psychometry, the ability to perceive information about an object through touch, intrigued me. I thought it would be marvelous to hold an object in my hands and be able to sense information about its owners and its past. My friend Mary Ann thought it would be marvelous, too, and one night she showed up with eight or ten objects to test my psychometric ability. As she handed me each one in turn—a bell, a doll's dress, a rhinestone brooch, a man's 1950's-style wristwatch—ideas instantly popped into my mind. Unfortunately, not one of them had anything to do with the object I was holding.

I was disappointed, but ever-cheerful Mary Ann said, "Look at it this way: it means you aren't just getting your psychic information by telepathy from the other person. If you were, you would have gotten information about every one of these objects from me." I was still disappointed, but she had a good point. Besides, I'm sure some practice wouldn't hurt.

When spirit communication was in vogue during the late 1800's and early 1900's, automatic writing was a popular way to receive messages from the Other Side. Automatic writing involves holding a pencil loosely and allowing it to form letters and words (or sitting at a keyboard and typing) with no prior knowledge of what will be written. The first time I attempted automatic writing, Patrice, a friend in England, had e-mailed to say she was giving up her four-year battle with ovarian cancer and moving into hospice care. She wrote that she hoped her friends and family would understand and wish her well on the next stage of her journey.

After the long battle, it was easy to understand her decision. I wanted to e-mail back and send her my love and support, but sitting at the computer, I had no idea what to say in such a difficult situation. Then it occurred to me to ask for spirit help. I placed my fingers lightly on the keyboard, sent Eia a silent plea for help, and started typing without the slightest conscious forethought.

The result was, well, interesting. It was sort of appropriate, but it sure wasn't anything I would have dared to write. In part, I'd typed, "Please know that your time here on Earth has been special, full of compassion and love for others and for yourself. ... Be gentle with yourself and wish yourself well on the journey home again. Know that you are going home, and your joy will be great when you arrive. Your hope for us who are left behind will be that we may join you soon, but we have more yet to accomplish, and we will be there soon enough. We will join you there when it is time. You will see us there. Thank you for your loving-kindness to us here on Earth and the love you will be sending us from the Other Side when you arrive. We love you, too, and send you on your way with joy. Thank you for sharing your time here with us. You bless us with your love. Amen."

I read it again and again, trying to decide where it had come from and whether I dared to send it. Was it a product of my own subconscious or imagination? It was clearly loving and positive, but would Patrice find it comforting? Or would she find it slightly stilted and odd, just as I did? In the end, I decided it must be from Eia since it surely didn't sound like me. I hit the send key.

I never had a reply from Patrice. According to an e-mail from her son, she passed away soon after. As for me, I gave up on automatic writing. After all, if spirits talk to you, why slow down the process by taking dictation?

The old thing about fortune tellers gazing into crystal balls turns out to be a real and time-honored technique for foretelling the future. Also called "scrying," it can be done by gazing into any reflective or luminescent surface such as crystal, water, or a mirror. In his book *Reunions*, the renowned expert on near-death experiences Raymond A. Moody, Jr., describes spirit encounters that have occurred while gazing into the depths of a mirror in a darkened room.

I purchased a medium-sized mirror and propped it on an easel so that it reflected only an empty spot on the ceiling. I turned off the lights, slowed my breathing, and spent perhaps eight hours over several days gazing into the depths of the mirror, hoping to zone out enough for a spirit communicator to appear. Having no luck, I invited my woo-woo friend Monica to join me so we could gaze into the mirror together. Probably because she actually sees spirits around her, Monica had considerably less tolerance than I had for sitting in the dark looking at nothing. After fifteen minutes she'd had enough, and I gave up, too, deciding I'd given it a fair try.

I also talked Monica into attempting physical mediumship with me. We placed a round pencil on the coffee table and concentrated on it with all our might, hoping to give it a psychic nudge, but the pencil never moved, and about five minutes of that was enough for Monica. Months later, over dinner in a restaurant, I suggested that maybe instead of just focusing on the pencil, we should have been asking our spirit guides to move it. Monica promptly unwrapped a fresh drinking straw and laid it on the table. Even though my hands were buzzing with energy, it was hard to muster any serious concentration in the middle of all the restaurant confusion, but we did give it a try. When the straw didn't move, Monica tried placing her hand about an inch above it to see if the energy from her palm would have any effect. Jerking her hand back, she rubbed her palm and looked at me indignantly. "I got zapped!" she said. "It was like a giant spark going right through my hand!" Placing my hand above the straw, I felt a couple of tiny twinges, but nothing resembling a zap. The straw never moved.

I wanted to try astral projection, too. Astral projection is an out-of-body experience in which the spirit leaves the physical body behind and retains consciousness as it travels over distances great or small, to a mountaintop in Peru or down the hall to the kitchen. I decided to start with the kitchen.

In books and on the web it's easy to find descriptions of how to accomplish astral projection. I went with the simplest, which suggests lying down, calming your mind, slowing your breathing, and simply "thinking yourself into" another location. My target was the kitchen, about fifteen feet down the hall from where I lay on my bed. On my fifth try, in my mind's eye I saw the dividers of a window pane, and looking down, I saw the top of my desk in my office across the hall. I'd missed my kitchen target, but my consciousness was *somewhere* my body was not. I wasn't, however, seeing my desk from the usual angle. Instead, it seemed as if I were floating above it with my head tipped slightly downward. It was a weird and uncomfortable view. I needed to take control and decided to try looking behind my computer monitor. Instantly I was *under* my computer table and looking out through the slats in the back of my desk chair. Strange indeed. Another instant, and I was viewing the office from a vantage point on the top shelf of the closet, looking out through the open closet doors.

I decided to see if I could think myself into the kitchen and look at the sink. I made it to the right room, but instead of looking at the sink, I saw a view across the kitchen island to the window above the dining room table. I tried to focus and pan my view over to the sink. It worked! But the view moved right past the sink and the stove and came to rest on the side of the refrigerator. I tried to think where I wanted to "go" next. I thought of Dad's house in Indiana, and instead found myself back in my body, lying on my bed. Curiouser and curiouser.

I haven't tried astral travel since because, frankly, I don't get the point. I've read that when you visit another location without your body, the people there can't see or hear you, and it seems to me like a terrible invasion of their privacy. What if I had succeeded in traveling to Dad's house and was able to prove it by telling him what I'd seen at that moment? If somebody did that to me, I would not be amused. Maybe someday I'll put my mind to it and see if I can send my consciousness somewhere peaceful and beautiful like a mountaintop, but even that seems a little pointless since you'd never be able to prove, even to yourself, that you were really there.

I *would* like to be able to read the future. At least, I think I would. Some psychics perceive information about their clients and can do just that, but I rarely receive that kind of message, and Eia very specifically tells people the future is not set in stone. Still, Monica and I agree it would be a handy ability to cultivate if one could. The problem is, you might never find out if your predictions came true, and even if they did, you might just be a lucky guesser. Someday we'll have to put our minds to it and give it a try. Maybe we do have the ability and just don't know it.

While I've never been lucky enough to see a spirit with my open eyes, I've had a few experiences that would be difficult to explain by the normal laws of nature. One night as I lay in bed waiting for sleep, there was a crash in the kitchen that sounded like something fell onto the counter top. It didn't sound like anything broke, and Jock wasn't particularly startled, so I didn't bother to investigate. The next morning I found a large plastic container had fallen from the top of my kitchen cupboards and landed on the smooth cooktop of my stove. This wouldn't be particularly startling except that the plastic bin is fourteen inches long, so at least seven inches of it would have to be hanging over the cabinet top before its fall could be explained by gravity alone. I'm sure I would have noticed if it had been sticking halfway out before I went to bed. I suspect some spirit person gave it a nudge. Too bad I didn't get up and discover it in the night. Maybe the nudger was hanging around hoping for a visit.

About two weeks later, my clock radio blared and woke me out of a sound sleep. Though the alarm was still set to go off at 6:15 a.m., the clock read 11:04 p.m. I'd barely fallen asleep. I switched the alarm button to off, but the radio kept blasting. I switched it on and off, but the radio continued to play. All I could think was, "How am I going to get any sleep if the radio won't shut off?" Exasperated, I finally pulled the plug, re-set the clock and the alarm, and crawled back under the covers. It wasn't until the next morning that the idea of a spirit connection hit me. Then, of course, it seemed obvious. Somebody wanted to communicate, and I wasn't even with-it enough to realize it.

A few months later, I was staying with my friend Kathryn when I blew it again. I have a cell phone that I use only when I travel. One morning when I turned it on, it made the zoop-zoop-zoop noise that indicates the arrival of a new message. I flipped through the phone's menus and found one new voice message waiting for me. The message began with static, then, through the static, I heard a woman's voice say eight or ten unintelligible words. I played it again. I couldn't make out her words, so I played it for Kathryn who agreed there was no telling what the woman was saying. Since no one has my cell number unless I'm going to be meeting them at an airport, it had to be a wrong number. No sooner did I hit the delete button than I recalled that every description I'd ever read of spirit telephone messages described exactly what I'd just heard: static followed by a hard-to-decipher voice through the noise. Frantically, I called my cell phone company to find out if the message could be restored and was devastated when they told me it was gone for good.

Later the same day, as I checked my e-mail on Kathryn's computer, I blithely deleted five or six consecutive messages that all said "unknown" in both the sender and the subject fields. The risk of acquiring a virus is just too high to open messages from unidentified senders, especially on someone else's computer. Then I got to thinking. I've seen "nothing" in e-mail subject lines before, but I've never seen "unknown" for the sender. What would the sender's address be if an e-mail came from the Other

Side? I quickly called my e-mail provider and was told the messages were unrecoverable. I'd thoroughly deleted them, too.

Obviously I'm not even enough of a woo-woo to recognize a spirit message when it wakes me up in the middle of the night, drops things, or calls me on the telephone. To my spirit communicators I send my sincere apologies! Please give me another chance, and I promise not to delete you or hang up on you next time!

21

A t a time when I had only six or seven readings under my belt, my friend Hollie, a petite and vivacious schoolteacher, asked me to try to contact a teenager named Lisa. Lisa, who died during a high school sports activity, had a vast collection of figurines and stuffed toys of her favorite animal, and Hollie felt that if Lisa got in touch from the Other Side, surely she would send a picture of this animal as an identifier to prove the contact was real. I explained to Hollie that we don't get to dictate what the spirits use as identifiers, but they're often things that represent our connection to the spirit sender.

The first image I saw was a capital L. A good sign, but since I already knew the girl's name was Lisa, it didn't prove anything. Next I saw a bicycle, coasting downhill with a rider aboard. Finally, an envelope appeared, with a heart-shaped sticker on the flap.

I was delighted when Hollie told me that her husband, Bob, taught Lisa to ride a bike by helping her coast down a hill, but Hollie was doubtful. "That would be a link with Bob, not me," she pointed out, then admitted that she'd been present for the lesson. I interpreted the envelope with the heart as a beautiful symbol that Lisa was "sending" her love, but Hollie couldn't get over that Lisa hadn't sent the animal image she'd expected, so she doubted the whole message. I couldn't believe it. Of all the bezillions of images she could have sent, Lisa showed me a picture of someone coasting down a hill on a bicycle—a memory she and Hollie shared. So what if she hadn't showed me the unicorn or the butterfly or the giraffe?

It was maybe a year later when I agreed to do another reading for Hollie, but I told her she had to remember that we don't get to pick the identifiers the spirits send. We have to take what we're shown and consider whether it represents a particular person, event, or idea. Hollie was surprised. She thought you were *supposed* to set up a test for the spirit by choosing two or three things by which they must identify themselves.

It does seem like we ought to be able to ask a simple test question like, "What color was your husband's hair?" and get a simple answer, but spirits virtually never take the bait when we try to test them. Believe me, I'd appreciate a simple test question and answer as much as my clients would. But at least it's reassuring to know that more than a hundred years ago mediums faced the same perplexing experience. In his 1874 work *Book on Mediums, or, Guide for Mediums and Invocators*, Allan Kardec explained the spirits' unwillingness to be tested as a simple breech of etiquette on our part—asking an insultingly obvious question to which both we and the spirit already know the answer. If Grandma were standing here in the flesh, he reasoned, would she answer such a ridiculous question? I'm not sure I buy Kardec's justification, but I don't have any better explanation.

The first person who came through in Hollie's second reading was an unknown man named George, a tall man holding a small dog in his arms. George told Hollie, "Your dad's right here," and indeed he was, standing up out of a wheelchair and announcing, "I can walk now!" Though she didn't tell me in advance, Hollie had recently driven a classic car that was her dad's favorite model, and she wished she could let him know. Almost the first image that came through was of Hollie behind the wheel of a car, but instead of being thrilled, she demanded, "What color is it?" If I'd known she was hoping for a car-driving message when I got that picture, I would have strangled her for asking such a question, but instead I searched for an answer. I couldn't see the outside of the car, but the floor mats looked dark, perhaps a gray color, so I said "gray." The classic car was brown and white, so Hollie discounted the communication altogether. She really didn't have a sense of how miraculous it is that *any* message at all reaches us from the Other Side or how lucky we are to get the slightest detail in the images we receive. Just to see Hollie at the wheel of a car was a gift.

When Rajiv, a self-assured journalism student from India, came for a reading to inquire about a romantic relationship, Eia indicated that there were two women of interest and asked why the one in India was waiting for him. Eia told Rajiv the woman is near his age and lives in Mumbai with her parents. She and Rajiv have known each other since they were children. She receives news of him through family connections and follows his career. I saw a picture of her working at a computer in an open room with many desks and other people working nearby. Eia indicated that the woman is not a clerical worker, but writes her own material. She showed me a long dark braid down the woman's back and a black watch band on her wrist, then even spelled out a name, "Maya." Eia told Rajiv that the young woman would be interested in him if he returned to India, but she is a professional woman and would also be just fine on her own.

In fact, Rajiv did know a woman who lives in Mumbai with her parents, writes copy for television, has known him since childhood, might hear news of him through family connections, and has a long black braid. But he demanded to know whether the woman Eia referred to was Christian or Hindu. Eia said that she, like Rajiv, is Christian. For Rajiv, that proved Eia was not describing the woman he knew, because she's Hindu, and besides, he told me, her name is Maga, not Maya!

When I heard from Rajiv a few months later, he told me he was certain that Maga could not have been the woman Eia was talking about because she is still a practicing Hindu and is now happily engaged to someone else. In my book, that was an incredibly detailed description to write off on the basis of one letter of her name and one error in detail. And I guess Rajiv forgot that Eia said the woman would be interested in him *if* he returned to India. I'm sure he had no idea how unusually detailed Eia's description was compared to a typical reading.

By all means, be skeptical of any purported message from a departed loved one or a spirit guide, and do insist on identifiers to validate who's sending the message, but keep your mind open and your brain in gear so you'll be able to recognize the connections that are real. And don't insist on an unreasonable level of detail. If you want Grandpa to know you ate an ice cream cone and he comes through with a picture of an ice cream cone, don't ask what flavor! It must take a huge amount of energy and effort for a spirit to communicate from the Other Side. If it were easy, surely they'd come through loud and clear with every detail.

And remember that the spirit has one whopping huge handicap: he has to work through the medium's brain to get his message across. He has to figure out what he can show me to get me to say the words that will be meaningful to you. It's exactly like playing charades. As I told Hollie, you might be hoping your mother will come through and call you Honeybear, but if she shows me a bear and a pot of honey, *I'm* going to say, "Pooh!"

22

I f there were skeptics, there were also believers, and I was amazed by the number of people who were eager to tell me about visions and visitations, flickering lights, long lost objects that suddenly reappeared, unexplained whiffs of a loved one's scent, and even near-death experiences. As I listened, I sensed the unspoken questions in the back of every mind: "Could *I* be a psychic? Could *I* receive messages from the dead? Talk to animals? Direct healing energy?" I'm convinced that everyone receives spirit and animal messages. It's just that they look and sound and feel exactly like our own imagination, so we fail to recognize them when we get them.

Sometimes people go in search of their psychic abilities, and sometimes their abilities come looking for them. My smart and funny journalist friend, Jennifer, called me for a reading one day. She was getting positively spooked because for several weeks streetlights had been blinking off and on as she passed under them. It didn't matter if she was on foot or in a car. Even her friends were noticing and wondering what was going on. It was weird. But Eia put Jennifer's mind at ease, telling her that a spirit guide named David was offering her the opportunity to channel him. The streetlights were his way of getting Jennifer's attention. He got it, all right! The next time a couple of us got together to practice channeling, Jennifer joined us and brought through a loving message from David on the very first try.

The more people I worked with and encouraged, the more it seemed that anyone with a serious and sincere interest discovered an ability to communicate with spirits, direct healing energy, or talk with animals. Natalie, the teenager who'd experienced fainting spells, began to perceive messages from her two horses. My friend Peggy, already an experienced healer, began to channel and easily received messages from her own guide Elizabeth, from my guide Eia, and even from my mother.

When I spoke at the Tanner Symposium on Religion and Culture, my friend Monica's hands tingled and buzzed as she listened. "You're a healer," I told her over lunch after my talk. Sure enough, as she tuned in to the energy in her hands, she found she could relieve her father's longstanding shoulder pain and ease the pain of a colleague's knee surgery. Her sister felt waves of energy from Monica's hands traveling from her head to her feet and back again.

It wasn't long before Monica began seeing spirits and hearing their messages during her healing work. When we got together to practice, I challenged her to try to contact someone named Lenore. I didn't tell her Lenore was my mother. Instantly Monica saw the image of a 1960's-style aluminum Christmas tree. I thought of Mom's parents' aluminum tree decorated entirely with red satin ornaments, ornaments my dad now hangs on his Christmas tree. The next thing Monica said was, "I see red polka dots. They're on the tree!"

As Monica and I practiced together, her psychic abilities continued to reveal themselves. She became aware of the presence of her own spirit guide, Michael. She saw my aura and my guide Eia around me. At a funeral she sensed and heard the deceased as he laughed about the mourners standing out in the rain on his account. One night when they were alone, Monica's friend Clark suddenly said, "What the heck is that?" when he saw little golden lights shooting from the back of her neck. He quickly explained it away as the reflections of the nightlight, but Monica knew better. When we asked Eia about the lights, she told us spirits often connect with our systems through the back of our necks. The little lights were the energy of the many spirits working with Monica, expressing their joy and responding to her joy as well.

I had no idea why my own psychic abilities had suddenly been revealed to me, so I simply asked Eia, "Why me?" and she replied, "Because you are a good communicator, you are manifestly open and honest, and your academic credentials will make it difficult for others to dismiss your experiences out of hand."

"So I'm a messenger?" I asked. "Why did it take so long to get to this point in my life?"

"There's no rush," Eia replied. "Your purpose in life is to get your message out. Your purpose is not to heal many people. Your purpose is to open their minds."

"So why am I doing healing work?" I asked.

"The healing is a vehicle to bring people news of the world that surrounds them, of which they are all a part, the flow of humanity—the flow of spirit—the flow of the universe—the flow of God's love."

"Still, I'd like to be a better healer, a better channel, a better medium," I told her.

"You will grow better with time," Eia told me, "as you write, as you bring your message into the light so people may examine it and understand what your experience has been."

I'd kept notes on my experiences since Mom's very first message. Still, I wasn't sure I really had a story to tell. "I don't know, Eia," I said. "It seems that to be credible bringing a message like that, I need to be a better medium."

"As your work progresses on Earth, your abilities will grow stronger," Eia told me. "You'll have more opportunities to channel, and channeling is your real gift. Mediumship is important and can touch many people, but this is not the real gift that you bring to the world. You're a messenger, a messenger asking human beings to open their minds, to listen to their hearts. Your ability to convey this message, your communication skill, is the characteristic that enables you to fulfill this assignment."

"Just to be clear," I said, "what precisely is the message that I'm supposed to convey by talking about my spiritual experiences?"

"There are more things in heaven than are dreamt of in your philosophy," Eia said, paraphrasing Shakespeare's Hamlet.

"That's it?" I asked.

"Open their minds. Let in the light. That's it."

"But what am I supposed to *say*?" I wondered.

"Tell them there's great goodness all around you," Eia replied. "Man is not alone. Human beings are not alone. They are part of a continuum of soul travel that was underway before they came to this life and continues when you lay down your body and are transformed into your spirit self once more. Tell them that human beings are here to practice kindness and acceptance and to banish fear from their own lives and from the lives of others. Do unto others as you would have others do unto you. Share the gift of goodness that is life. Life is not hard; it is a gift. It is a short gift, an opportunity to grow spiritually and to experience yourself as love."

23

My friend Monica, whose spiritual abilities blossomed so quickly, was the very same person God had addressed as she lay on my healing table, calling her "My beloved child in whom I am well pleased" and telling her the pain in her elbow would vanish. Two months later Monica's grown son Chase became the second person God spoke to through me.

Chase made an appointment for a reading with Eia, and as I prepared for his visit, I clicked a cassette into the tape recorder, cleared my mind, and thanked God for His gift of spirit communication. I closed my eyes and visualized God and my spirit helpers ranged in a semicircle before me. As I greeted each one in my mind—God, Mom, Eia, Dr. Nu, Roger, Williams—I thanked them for their assistance and asked for their help so that I might be a clear receiver and an accurate translator of Eia's words.

It was a ritual I always followed to calm my mind for healing or psychic work, but this time something was different. The portion of the semicircle that I visualize as being occupied by God began to expand and soon filled the entire screen of my mind while the spirit helpers receded into the background. I got the feeling God was taking over the conversation, so I addressed Him in my mind. *Are You telling me that the message for Chase will be from You and not from Eia?* I asked.

God's gentle voice answered, "Now you understand Me."

I was alarmed. It was one thing to bring through a few loving remarks during a healing session, but I definitely didn't want either the responsibility or the reputation for channeling God. I suggested that perhaps I could start the session with Eia and if it became clear that God was speaking, I could say to Chase, "Well, by golly, it seems that God has some things to say to you as well."

"Don't worry," God reassured me.

"Well, how am I supposed to explain this to Chase?" I asked.

"You're good at explaining things," came the serene reply. Just in case we really did hear from God, I set up a second tape recorder.

When Chase arrived we chatted about my spiritual work and Chase's own mystical experiences. Finally I told him what had happened as I prepared for his reading. I told him that as crazy as it sounded, I *thought* what we were about to hear was a message for him from God. Then I added hopefully, "Or maybe not!"

When I channel Eia, my voice doesn't change, but Chase told me afterwards that as God's words came through, my voice was more forceful and a bit deeper than ordinary. To me it sounded more serene.

My nervousness was obvious as I began the tape, saying, "This is a reading for Chase, and the date is Tuesday, January 18th, 2005. Okay, um, well, um, God, why don't You go ahead and begin—and begin wherever You want to begin."

God began with the phrase that signaled His presence. "Chase, you are My beloved son, in whom I am well pleased. You are strong and strong-hearted and full of love. I send you My best blessings, and I tell you that I am your Father, and you are My son. You have done well in everything that you have undertaken. You have made difficult choices with great wisdom, and I am proud of you.

"When you are fearful of the choices that life places before you, your fear stems from your lack of understanding of who you really are. You are My holy child. You can do no wrong. No harm can come to you. …

"I'm speaking to you tonight for two reasons. The first is to tell you that any idea you harbor about punishment from on high, from God, is a figment of your imagination. There is nothing but love for you here and throughout all of eternity. I'm calling to you now that you might release the burden of your belief that there are right and wrong choices to be made. I tell you now, every choice is right. This is My will for you and for all of humanity: that you should experience the great joy of knowing who you really are through the choices you make, revealing yourself to yourself. I tell you, you are nothing but light, pure energy, pure love, pure forgiveness for others, pure goodness, and your only purpose on this Earth is to discover and to experience the truth of who you really are.

"You have nothing to gain by judging yourself harshly. Such judgments are imposed upon yourself by yourself and certainly not by Me, for I love you no matter what you do. If I were to give you choices and condemn you for choosing one thing rather than the other, that would be no freedom of choice. Truly, you have complete freedom of choice, and there are no negative consequences attached. No judgment from Me will ever be meted out.

"Your religions have taught you to believe in a vengeful god, a god who exacts punishment for imagined wrongs. I want to be very clear: there is nothing you can do that will hurt Me. There is nothing I need from you, nothing I require of you.

"I have said that I am talking to you for two reasons tonight, first to assure you that there is no judgment attached to any decision you make in this life. The second reason I am talking to you tonight is to assure you that you are blessed, you are My holy child, and I hold you close to My heart. I enfold you in My embrace. I hold you on My lap. I hold you to My breast, and I want you to feel in your own heart the utter and complete love that I have for you. You are My son, in whom I am well pleased.

"I cannot say this any more clearly than to repeat these two messages to you. First, there are no wrong decisions. It is through the choices you make that you will discover who you truly are, that you will unfold the great goodness, the light, the healing energy that is in your touch, the love that you bring to yourself and to the world around you. Savor your choices and enjoy making them, knowing that you make them in complete safety and with My great love and for My pleasure at watching you discover the greatness of who you truly are.

"My second message is that I wish to tell you verbally—as a way of encouraging you to experience emotionally and at a soul level—how deeply, thoroughly, ultimately you are loved by Me. Nothing can ever come between us. It is impossible for us to be separated from one another, and you are enveloped in My love from start to finish, alpha to omega, beginning to end. You are My great love.

"... I send you My peace and My blessing, and I thank you for the great joy you give Me. Enjoy the experience of living and always know that you are safe and you are loved by Me. Amen."

When the message ended, Chase and I sat looking at each other, shaking our heads in amazement at the great love God had expressed. We laughed as I confessed that I'd been more than a little nervous about bringing through a message from God, and Chase told me, "You should have heard it from my seat! I've had a lifelong torment of God."

There were two big confirmations for me in Chase's reading. There were no surprises as God made His first point, that He does not judge us for our choices and decisions. The concept can be found in Neale Donald Walsch's *Conversations with God* books. But as God spoke, my mind raced, and I thought I knew what His second point would be. Afterwards, I couldn't remember what I'd expected, but it was nothing as simple as what came next: "I love you." I knew I wasn't making it all up, because if I were, the second message would have been something else entirely.

My second validation came when Chase suddenly said, "Do you want to hear something *really* wild? As you started speaking the message, my vision was brought to focus directly on your face. The rest of the room just went out of focus. I even tried to look down the hall and look at the dog, but I couldn't. Everything was out of focus except your face. It was like God was saying,

'Pay attention to *this*.' Then, as soon as you stopped talking, everything came back into focus."

I don't think you're supposed to question the message if God uses you for a mouthpiece, but I was still the tiniest bit disappointed. "To be honest," I told Chase, "there wasn't anything in that reading that I couldn't have made up."

"True," he agreed, "but you couldn't make your house disappear!"

In another disappearing act, Chase's tape recording of the session started and ended with *my* comments and was completely blank in between as God spoke. It's only because I ran two tape recorders that night that we have a record of God's loving message to Chase.

24

I t's striking to me," I said to God one day, "that You use the same words to describe people whom You address through me as You used to describe Jesus at His baptism."

"Why should I not?" God replied, "for you are truly all My sons and daughters, and it is impossible for you to do anything to displease Me."

"Why, then, don't You speak to everyone who comes to me for a reading?" I asked.

"Some people," He explained, "can hear and understand and accept messages from Eia who would be unable to comprehend or believe that God was speaking to them personally. It is for this reason that I speak through Eia."

It made a lot of sense to hear that God speaks through Eia, for her messages are deeply loving and supportive. I'd heard her talk to people about love, about loss, about family, about career. She brought messages from those who've passed on and offered guidance on people's spiritual paths. I'd heard her remind instead of scold and reassure rather than abandon. She is unfailingly kind. Once, when asked if a lover was in fact a married man, she responded gently, "Why do you want to be with someone you cannot trust?" When a frightened mother turned to her for help, Eia gently reminded her that even if her son should commit suicide, he would not die, but simply make the transition back to his natural state with God.

I wanted to know about suicide, too. Every spiritual book I'd read indicated that God disapproves of suicide. Some said that to commit suicide is to reject God's most holy gift, the gift of life.

Others said that the souls of those who commit suicide linger indefinitely in a gray and horrible limbo, unable to progress toward the light that is God and His love. I'd even read that those who commit suicide make a U-turn at heaven, immediately returning to Earth to master the lessons they've not yet learned. By all accounts, suicide results in God's grave displeasure.

But how could that be true? I'd heard God Himself say, "I do not judge you now or ever" and, "You can do nothing that would displease Me. There is nothing I need from you. Nothing is required." Dr. Nu said that the time to leave our human body is a decision negotiated between the soul and the mind. If it's our decision to come to Earth in a human incarnation, our decision to leave, and our option to return to future lifetimes, how could it be a sin to choose to leave an incarnation that has become unbearable? I'm not arguing in favor of suicide and the devastation that comes in its wake. In fact, I've done readings in which loved ones on the Other Side urged my clients to remember their responsibilities, reconnect with family members, and stop considering suicide. But I simply couldn't believe that God would *punish* us for throwing in the towel and beginning anew in some future lifetime. Surely an all-loving and compassionate God would not punish us for returning home to Him earlier than planned. Would He?

The question had been on my mind for months when a friend and an acquaintance's son committed suicide within two weeks of each other. Now it was personal. I had to know how God really felt about suicide, so I sat down one afternoon and cleared my mind. I took my time, breathing slowly and deeply. As I felt a quiet calm come over me at last, I thanked God for His gift of communication, and then asked Him outright, "God, please explain what happens to the spirits of those who commit suicide."

His answer was immediate. "They are welcomed home with open arms. There are no negative consequences." At last an answer that made sense to me, an answer of loving compassion from God Himself.

Just as Eia said that a heavenly message may come to you in the words of a book you're reading, a few days later I found confirmation of God's statement in John Edward's book *One Last Time*. John wrote that the suicides he's talked with are not in limbo and do not describe any negative consequences whatsoever.

Two years after Kristine's son Tom committed suicide and the pink childlike spirit appeared as I sent her healing energy, Kristine and I got together hoping to hear from Tom. He came through instantly, wanting his mother to know that he is at peace, joyful, well, happy, without fear, and in a beautiful place. He urged her to let go of the guilt she has been carrying and told her it's time to move on with her life. It's time to let go. When she asked what she should do with his ashes, Tom told her to put them on her rosebushes, which was exactly what Kristine had been contemplating.

Like Hillyard, whose descendants called him Hillard, Tom kept interrupting our conversation until I finally had to stop and tell Kristine, "You know, every time you say 'Tom,' I hear 'Thomas' in the other ear." She laughed and admitted that he always preferred to be called Thomas.

Thomas named and talked about his brother, an uncle, an aunt, a grandmother, and even the family dog—sending me the word "alligator," which turned out to be the little dog's nickname. Then he talked about his passing, saying that at the time he died, he'd been thinking about leaving but "wasn't quite there yet" when spirits came and told him it was time to go. They accompanied him, he said, and he had no pain or fear. It was an easy transition to the Other Side.

In the spirit world, Tom told us, he's assisting younger suicide victims who arrive on the Other Side abruptly, sometimes even to their own surprise. Because of his own experience, he says, he can help this special group.

The father of several grown children, a short, blond, and earnest man named Steven was a new and aspiring healer. He had always been a down-to-earth guy and was amazed when he began to feel healing energy surging through his body. Fascinated, he dedicated himself to learning how to utilize his new gift, yet in the midst of this exciting development in his life, he suddenly plunged into the depths of depression and despair. Even he was at a loss to explain the change, while friends and family wondered if some chemical in his work environment could have caused the abrupt and drastic change. And then he was gone, committing suicide after a family dinner, lying on the bed and putting a gun to his temple.

Several months later my friend Nyla called me for a reading. A paper with Steven's name on it had mysteriously disappeared out of her filing cabinet and reappeared on top of her antique Victrola phonograph. Little things had been disappearing and reappearing around the house, and this was the last straw.

As I settled my mind to begin the reading, I asked Eia if she would speak with Nyla. "I will speak second," she replied.

Surprised, I asked God if He would be speaking, and He answered, "I will speak through Eia." I hesitated, not sure who, then, was going to speak first.

Suddenly Steven appeared in my mind's eye, right in front of me as if I could reach out and touch him. He was grinning and waving with both hands. "Hi!" he said with obvious joy. Then to Nyla he said, "I knew I could get you to go to Jan!" He told us life is wonderful on the Other Side. He's doing healing work both there and on Earth and loving every moment. He was glowing with happiness.

When Nyla asked if there was anything she could do for Steven's wife, he thanked her for all she'd already done and simply said that his wife would be fine. We were taken aback by his apparent lack of concern, but he clearly was confident that she would survive and be all right.

Nyla asked Steven what caused his seemingly sudden depression and suicide. "Was it some sort of chemical at work?" she asked.

"No, they came and got me!" he exclaimed. "They tapped me on the shoulder and said, 'You're outta here!'" As he said it, I saw a vision of four tall, white-robed figures surrounding him. Sure enough, one of them tapped him on the shoulder, then jerked a thumb heavenward as if to say, "You're outta here!" His description bore a striking resemblance to Thomas's statement that he'd thought of suicide but "wasn't quite there yet" when the spirits came and told him it was time to go.

I can't explain how "They came and got me" squares with loading a gun, putting it to your head, and pulling the trigger. Still, both men gave the same description, so I guess I have my answer about suicide. Both Steven and Thomas declared that spirits came to claim them, the transition was easy, and they're thrilled with their new work on the Other Side. And after all, God Himself had said those who commit suicide are welcomed home with open arms.

25

Divorce is hard, and it's a long transition, getting your feet back under you and rebuilding your life. Long after my new house was stocked with the basics of laundry detergent and wastebaskets and cookware, long past the period of unexpected discoveries like "I don't have measuring cups!" I remember the day I went to the bookstore to purchase a thesaurus. I selected a small paperback edition because it was cheap. I paid for it and walked out to the car. I climbed in, took out the thesaurus, and stared at the tiny print. *This is ridiculous,* I thought. *I'm a grownup adult woman, and this is my thesaurus. I'm going to own it for the rest of my life, and I deserve a decent hardback copy.* I marched back into the store and traded the thrifty edition for a hefty tome I'll never need a magnifying glass to read. When I got home I took our wedding silverware out of the closet and made room for it in the silverware drawer. Then I got on the internet and ordered myself two springform pans and a set of 500 thread count sheets. On that day I transcended post-divorce survival mode and reclaimed my life.

My life is not about salvage work or finding someone to complete me. I *am* complete. My life is about knowing myself, working to improve, learning everything I can, and trying my best to be kind. My connections to family are stronger than ever. Frank and I see each other when we take turns dog sitting, and he has a new love in his life. I'm slowly inching my chair closer to the goldfinches at my bird feeder and pondering whether, with red lipstick and a mouthful of sugar water, I could entice a hummingbird to give me a kiss.

Dad's World War II pain has never returned, and Mom continues to communicate with me, not only in conversations when I sit still long enough to listen, but through little gifts delivered right to my door. Every so often I open my front door and find a tiny bluebird feather, a yellow willow leaf, or a flower precisely in the center of my welcome mat. Once there was a little apricot. Before my woo-woo adventures, I hardly would have noticed.

And what about my spiritual adventures? Where are they leading me? I have no idea, but I'm certainly enjoying the journey. The skeptics, whose arguments all boil down to, "I don't believe it; therefore it's impossible," are on their own journeys and will find their own truth. All I can do is tell you what my experience has been.

I still struggle to believe I really can get messages from the Other Side, and sometimes I feel like quitting my spirit work altogether because it's not fun to know people think you're loopy and to always feel you have to explain yourself. But then some spirit sends an irrefutable identifier like "totem pole" or Eia answers a question before it's even asked. How can I argue with that? I'm still fascinated by every single communication from the spirit world, and I'm constantly struck by the depth of love that enfolds us even when we're unaware of it. Virtually every experience on my spiritual journey has been positive and full of loving support for us as human beings.

When people shake their heads and tell me I have a gift, I assure them they have the same gift just waiting to be discovered. God's loving-kindness, His angels, and His spirit helpers surround us all. Open up to the unseen world. You already recognize unseen energies; you believe in sound waves and light waves, germs, gravity, magnetism, x-rays, atoms and molecules, and the ultraviolet light that gives you a sunburn. Know that, truly, "There are more things in Heaven and Earth than are dreamt of in your philosophy." Slow down and make time for new experiences. Read and explore new ideas. Reflect thoughtfully, and discover what rings true to you. Calm your mind and your spirit. Reach out to God, your loved ones on the Other Side, and the spirit helpers who support you. Believe in the communication you receive, even when it feels like your own imagination. If it is loving and good, give it the benefit of the doubt. Listen and consider the truth of it. God does not just speak to saints. He speaks to you.

And what does God say to us? "I love you. I love you all. Nothing can separate you from My love. We are one. You are My holy child, and you are safe. There is no force for evil in the world. You are mine, and I will not forsake you. Indeed, we could not be separated from each other if you tried. You are a gift to yourself and to the world. You are holy. Savor the experience of revealing yourself to yourself, and do not fear. I am with you. I could not be otherwise. Enjoy the ride, and I will welcome you home when you return. You are all My beloved children, in whom I am well pleased. Amen."

ACKNOWLEDGMENTS

Many people have helped and encouraged me along my woo-woo path, and I'm grateful to every one of them. Mom, of course, tops this list as the person and spirit who opened the door to my spiritual experiences and pushed me through it. Dad is next on the list, for letting me follow Mom's laying-on-hands instructions barely a week after her very first message. Special thanks go to my brothers, David and Bob, for not calling the booby hatch. And I can never sufficiently thank my dear friend Monica Ingold, the person who has shared and practiced and learned with me almost from the beginning of this path.

I'm indebted to the many people who trusted me to contact their loved ones on the Other Side, to talk with their pets, and to share healing energy with them—and then gave me permission to write about their experiences in these pages. Some of their names have been changed at their request.

Others graciously gave me feedback on my work as I wrote. Nancy Williams and Jeri Malouf were especially helpful.

My heartfelt thanks to all who have given me their assistance and support. And, of course, I thank God or the Universe—whatever you choose to call that Spirit of Love which gives us the gift of life and the gift of self-awareness that enables us to love and to grow.